D1560238

Coming Home to Mississippi

Coming Home
to Mississippi

Edited by

Charline R. McCord and Judy H. Tucker

UNIVERSITY PRESS OF MISSISSIPPI

JACKSON

www.upress.state.ms.us

The University Press of Mississippi is a member
of the Association of American University Presses.

First printing 2013

∞

Library of Congress Cataloging-in-Publication Data

Coming home to Mississippi / edited by Charline R. McCord and Judy H. Tucker.
    p. cm.
  ISBN 978-1-61703-766-5 (cloth : alk. paper) — ISBN 978-1-61703-767-2 (ebook) 1. American
literature—Mississippi. I. McCord, Charline R. II. Tucker, Judy H.
  PS558.M7C66 2013
  810.8'09762—dc23   2012033122

British Library Cataloging-in-Publication Data available

Contents

5

Introduction

Charline R. McCord and Judy H. Tucker

Coming Home to Mississippi is the companion to our earlier collection *Growing Up in Mississippi*. *Growing Up* aspires to tell the reader what makes a Mississippian, to somehow explain the influences within the state that propel our citizens of the world to accomplish so much.

Coming Home examines Mississippians' comings and goings—why they leave, where they go, what they do there, and why they always know in their bones they will be back some day. As editors, we have a vested interest in this subject; we too ventured out of state, lingered a while, and then came on back home. We talk about these journeys in our own essays in this volume.

Sometimes a change of venue can be helpful, and certainly it's an admirable goal to learn all you can, become a citizen of the world, understand other regions and cultures, and prove to yourself that you can make it anywhere. These are exciting ways to expand your horizons, fill your time, and build the all-important life resume so that, as Thoreau said, when you come to die you won't discover that you have not lived. Yet, there is such comfort in knowing there's a home, however humble, waiting for you in the mystique that is Mississippi—a place where change is subjected to due diligence, where new ideas have to be assessed, juried, and found necessary before they're accepted. Mississippi is a land where we don't spend a lot of time worrying about fixing things that aren't broken. So there's a good chance, if you do venture out, that when you come on back you'll find most everything right where you left it.

Our people have left for many different reasons. There was the migration to the North in hopes of a better, freer, more dignified life for many. The oil fields and the wheat fields of the West promised better wages. The creative among us dreamed of making it in Nashville or Hollywood or New York. And they did too! They made it on the big screen and the big stage, in editing, publishing, and writing, in sports, in politics. As we send this book to press, Brandon's own Skylar Laine is tearing up the stage as a top five contestant on *American Idol*. Will she come home to Mississippi? In a dirt road minute!

Some of our writers left because of civil rights, some left to protect our rights, and others fled from Katrina. There are family separations and couple separations—one who left in a swirl of civil rights and personal rights thought she could never return. But Norma Watkins did come back, and she was welcomed at Lemuria to sign copies of her moving and highly successful memoir.

One of our essayists felt so strongly about getting away he proclaimed, "I'm leaving and I ain't never coming back!" But God had other plans for Dolphus Weary; he's back, and he's doing great work through his ministry. We're glad you changed your mind, Dr. Weary. Mississippi needs your voice.

A few of our writers—Mary Ann Mobley, Bill Dunlap, Jerry Ward, Morgan Freeman, Sela Ward—maintain a dual residency, yo-yoing in and out of Mississippi because their heartstrings are tied firmly here, but some spinoff part of their lives still demands their partial presence elsewhere.

Morgan Freeman, Sam Haskell, Mary Donnelly, David Sheffield, Cynthia Walker, Sela Ward, and Marco St. John left to become stars and they all hit home runs on the fields of Hollywood and New York. But when they got homesick, the only cure was to come on back home, where they could breathe the right air, walk the right land, and sit on the right front porch. Today, technology allows them to ply their trades right from their own special Mississippi space.

Most of us have heard the story of William Faulkner's 1940s experience in Hollywood as a screenwriter for MGM studios. It seems that after a period of time spent trying to write in a sterile office provided to him by MGM, Faulkner told director Howard Hawks that he would be more comfortable writing at home. Hawks gave him permission to do that, and when he hadn't heard from Faulkner for several days he phoned his hotel to see how the writing was coming along. But Faulkner had checked out. When he said home, he meant *home*, and Howard Hawks learned Faulkner was back in Mississippi, where he belonged.

Mississippians don't need a GPS to find their way back. Did you know a GPS won't even work in the Mississippi Delta? While our reasons for leaving the state are myriad, our reasons for coming home are pretty much the same: Mississippi is heavy on our minds, in our hearts, and in our blood. This state encompasses who we are, what we love, where we find comfort, and where we belong.

Coming Home
to Mississippi

William Dunlap

William Dunlap of Webster County is a peripatetic artist who maintains studios in McLean, Virginia, Coral Gables, Florida, and Mathiston, Mississippi. His paintings, sculpture, and constructions can be found in a broad array of public and private collections. The University Press of Mississippi recently published a comprehensive monograph titled *Dunlap*, and there is more than you ever wanted to know on the website www.williamdunlap.com.

We expatriate Mississippians carry with us a burden of history and memory that would be far harder to bear were there not so many of us out there that the mathematical probability of our running into one another, anywhere on the planet, remains extremely high.

In 1996 I was in Hanoi working on an exhibition of contemporary art from that troubled land which would travel throughout the United States. Our two nations had not had diplomatic relations since 1974, but things were slowly changing. Overseeing this delicate process was a man who was a legend in the State Department—Chargé d'Affaires Desaix Anderson of Sumner, Mississippi. We had never met, but Desaix had been most forthcoming in our correspondence. As an artist himself and fluent in Vietnamese, he was poised to be a great deal of use to my project.

I turned up at the appointed time at his four-story town house in a leafy residential area of Vietnam's capital with an appropriate gift—a duty-free bottle of Jack Daniel's. We climbed to his rooftop terrace, raised our glasses, and looked out over this French colonial city with all its recent and ancient history and talked about the Delta. Not the Mekong Delta, mind you, but our great mutual Mississippi Delta and all the people and places we had in common. It was a transporting and memorable conversation, but not a unique one.

I haven't lived in Mississippi for some four decades now, but in a very real sense I have never left. Any excuse to come home has always been a good one. Family, friends, football and funerals have kept me coming back with alarming regularity.

Then there is the land and the small piece of it I have retained in Webster County. This is where the Natchez Trace crosses the Big Black River in north Mississippi hill country. In the early nineteenth century ancestors of mine arrived in droves after the Treaty of Dancing Rabbit Creek opened the rich bottomlands for cultivation and the hardwood forests for harvest. They hunkered down, worked hard, praised the Lord, worshipped education, and made whiskey and a fine life for themselves.

During a recent fall, I had the self-indulgent pleasure of spending an extended period of time in the great Magnolia State. I occupied the Starnes House in Mathiston and worked in the converted Church of Christ that is my studio. A number of art exhibitions and book signings kept me riding the roads from one end of the state to the other: Memphis to New Orleans, Greenwood and Greenville, on to Starkville, Hattiesburg, Oxford, Holly Springs, Tutwiler, Morton, Forest, Bellefontaine, New Albany, Tupelo, Laurel, and all points in between.

For me, something quite close to absolute clarity can occur while driving these roads. I do some of my best thinking behind the wheel and many a painting has been first glimpsed in my mind's eye as the landscape slides by at a high rate of speed, adult beverage close at hand.

Mississippi has changed immensely since my youth, but much of it, the best of it, has remained the same. Its physical beauty is as rich, subtle, and seductive as ever. While we're not much affected by seasons, this particular autumn was one of the most electrifying and colorful in living memory. The sumac and poison ivy were fire red, the oak and sweet gum orange as a setting sun, and copper-colored broom sedge stretched as far as the eye could see. It was not lost on me. Nor were all the sites, situations, air, and light that have helped inform a life's work as a painter.

Bumping along on I-55 between Canton and Jackson, I recalled a college-era summer job that had me and some buddies building this very stretch of interstate through Madison County. (I expect this explains the still rough ride.) I also knew this sublimely pastoral landscape from plein air painting excursions with Dr. Sam Gore of Mississippi College. Nissan's state-of-the-art production plant now occupies the place, and a large painting of mine embracing both incarnations of this landscape hangs in their lobby. Stop in and have a look sometime.

Our greatest memoirist, Willie Morris, often said, "Mississippi is not a state. It's a club." A club, to be sure, and one that provides many a privilege, not the least of which is the unearned intimacy that can occur when you hear a stranger speak in a strange land and recognize that he's not just from your general place, the U.S. of A., but from a special part of your place—this complicated commune called Mississippi. So you introduce yourself and pretty soon you are finishing each other's sentences and learning, to no one's surprise, that all of you just might be kin, once or twice removed.

Club Mississippi comes with specific, if minimal, requirements for entrance. Birthplace helps, though it's not mandatory. Intellectual curiosity and a sense of history will take you a long way. A tolerance for narrative is a must. But do know that this club is an all-consuming lifetime commitment, and, try as you might, your fees will never be paid in full.

I qualify, thank God, and am damned proud to be a member, even if I am constantly behind in my dues.

Morgan Freeman

Morgan Freeman was born in Memphis in 1937, but grew up in Charleston and Greenwood, Mississippi. He is a major film actor who has performed in some ninety-four movies, as well as being a director, an aviator, and the owner of Ground Zero Blues Club, located in Clarksdale, Mississippi. He has won a Golden Globe, a Screen Actor's Guild Award, and an Oscar for his work in *Million Dollar Baby*, and the 2012 Golden Globe Awards honored him with the prestigious Cecil B. DeMille Award for outstanding contributions to the world of entertainment. He is also the founder of the Rock River Foundation charity fund.

I grew up in a segregated society, but I never gave it much thought until I was older. That was just the way life was for us at the time.

Most of my friends and family were never concerned about why we had to sit in the balcony of the Paramount Theater; we simply wanted to see the movies. It was obvious blacks attended separate schools, but our parents were just as concerned about our grades as the white parents were. It never occurred to me to demand admission to the floor seats in the theater or entrance into the white schools. I never thought much about things being separate. I just accepted life in Mississippi for what it was and lived accordingly. Yet I never lost sight of the fact that, despite my family and my love for them, I wanted to leave Mississippi and never return.

In the dusty haze of those hot Mississippi Delta summer days I saw myself as an airplane pilot; I dreamed of seeing new places and meeting people who accepted me on my own merits and not the amount of money in my pockets. I knew there was a big world out there beyond the shimmering fields, and I couldn't wait to get out in it and make my mark via whatever means I could. I figured that even if I wasn't able to make a name for myself, my main goal was to simply get out of Mississippi.

My ticket out was the U.S. Air Force, and it was with a naïve optimism and boundless hope that I joined up and left the state, I presumed, for good.

Funny how things turn out. How true the adage "life is what happens while you're making other plans."

The air force gave me perspective, to say the least. It was there that for the first time I experienced a new kind of racism. Back in Mississippi, a person knew where he stood: racism was out in the open, an "in-your-face" strain of segregation and denied civil rights. What I encountered upon leaving the state, however, was a more deceptive form, more or less under the table and more institutionalized. Leaving Mississippi made me realize that the South certainly had no corner on the market when it came to racism and segregation. I came to realize that, given a choice, I would rather deal with someone who is up front about their beliefs—no matter how distasteful—than someone who pretends to be an ally only to then set about undermining your progress behind your back. In the North, I encountered racism that was insidious and painful. I wanted to think I was freer there, but I was not.

In some strange way, leaving Mississippi was what enabled me to feel the first sort of pride for the place. At the very least, our people were frank and open in regards to who and what we were. There was certainly no pretentiousness in that regard. The idea of a "New South" where equal opportunity abounded was never subscribed to by my home state. We were what we were, and the rest of the country could be damned. Once I got a sense of how racism was manifested "out there" it gave me some comfort to know at least Mississippi was honest about it.

What was true then is true now: Mississippi is in fact no more or no less racist than the rest of the country.

The ensuing years found most of my family leaving Mississippi as well. They all had their own reasons for leaving, and I of course cannot speak for them in regards to why they left. In 1956—or maybe it was

'57—however, my parents returned. I was stunned by their decision, and I couldn't fathom why they would want to return.

I was on leave when I came to pay a visit in 1957. They were living in a pitiful shack where my beautiful house now stands. I thought, my, how bad things must have gotten for them in Nashville, for when I left they had a couple of businesses and were seemingly making great headway.

When I came back some nine years later they had done what they had meant to do all along. Built a nice four-bedroom house where my office now stands today. How idyllic it looked to me back then.

Twenty-five years after I had left Mississippi for good, I started re-considering my general feelings about the state. By then I had started achieving a modicum of success in my acting career, and over the next few years I would occasionally return to Mississippi to visit my parents. What I found during those visits was surprising. I would sit on the porch of their little house in the Mississippi Delta and gaze out across the fields onto the lush green landscape, listening to the birds and frogs, basking in the heat and humidity, and I felt a peace. Far from the smog and the frenetic pace, far from high prices and the even higher personal demands of living in the compression of a large city, I came to realize that I harbored a true love of place, Mississippi. The people I encountered on the streets were more sincere, courteous, and helpful. In a very short time they came to accept me as a friend instead of a celebrity. I realized early on that I was proud of my Mississippi roots, and that there were plenty of reasons for that pride.

It was during those visits that I started thinking about coming home.

By the 1980s my career had taken hold, and I was finally landing roles I once only dreamed of. My parents were aging, however, and I found myself spending more and more of my free time in Mississippi. I guess it was around that time that my wife, Myrna Colley-Lee, decided that we wanted to build a home there. My parents had already told me that I was to inherit a goodly portion of the property so we proceeded to build right on the spot where I first saw them living in that pitifully rundown house when I came back to visit in the midfifties. Many of my friends were shocked that we were settling down in Mississippi.

They would ask, "Why do you want to live in Mississippi?" Even many Mississippians asked it. "You can live anywhere in the world you want. Why Mississippi?" My response: "Because I can live anywhere I want." It is a source of pride for me to reclaim my state. I had left for greener pastures, found them, and mined them. In time I discovered that my parents owned the greenest pasture right here in our ancestral home, the Mississippi Delta.

Our home is built on that land, with a few more acres added for horses, a pond, and a necessary gate for privacy. It's a couple of steps up from the shotgun house I was raised in. My wife, a costume designer, spends much of her downtime digging in the rich Delta soil, landscaping, and gardening. My parents have now both passed away, but they rest nearby in the family cemetery located on the property. Their house still stands and serves as my office and home for my assistant. Our granddaughter, E'dena, came to live with us and I was proud to give her the opportunity to embrace her Mississippi roots as she grew into a lovely, intelligent, and talented young woman.

So while I admittedly could not wait to leave, one of the smartest moves I have made in life is to come back home. Mississippi is the first place I truly embraced as a professional and as a friend. When the state legislature paid tribute to my achievements a few years ago, I found myself flooded with emotion and pride. Standing in there, in the capitol in Jackson, I realized it was a long way from those days in the balcony at the Paramount in Greenwood, and it hit home just how far my state and I have come since those days.

Does that mean I claim Mississippi is perfect? Not by any means. Does that mean I believe we don't have more work to do? Not at all. But what all this does mean to me is that our state is no longer a poster child for racism and ignorance. It means that Mississippi is just like every other place on earth, trying to acknowledge and deal with its past while moving forward with the conviction that mistakes won't be repeated.

At times young people approach me, asking why I returned to Mississippi. Many—just like me when I was younger—say they cannot wait to leave here and never return. I have to admit that I don't discourage their leaving. However, I do point out that they need to reconsider never returning. I think it is wise for our youth to get out in the world, to experience new things, people of varying backgrounds, and the different ways of viewing all that life has to offer. I tell them to do all of that—chances are many of them will then come home.

Since returning to Mississippi I have been fortunate to meet Bill Luckett and become a partner in Madidi, a fine dining establishment, and Ground Zero Blues Club, a "juke joint," located in Clarksdale. In four short years, we have seen Clarksdale and the Mississippi Delta grow as an international tourist destination. While blues aficionados once trickled in and out of Clarksdale, we now have in place a burgeoning tourism-driven economy. Other businesses have opened to meet tourists' needs, and we all try to work together to promote all the great things we know we have to offer in the Delta, specifically—and Mississippi in general. More and more, we are seeing people move from other areas into the state. More and more of our own that have chosen to leave return home as well.

What I often hear from visitors is, "Mississippi isn't anything like I expected." This is always said with a surprised smile.

We are slowly but surely winning a public relations battle with our past. When people come to our cities and businesses, they see people from all backgrounds, all walks of life, and all economic strata, working and enjoying life—together. When they meet our people, they realize that they are our biggest assets. Mississippians are helpful, generous, polite—and often funny as hell. We also know how to have a real good time.

One of our employees who works with the media always tells us that we should lobby to have the state slogan changed from "Mississippi—The Hospitality State" to "Mississippi—It Ain't What You Think." She does so only half jokingly. Mississippi has changed, and we now know that if we can get a person here just once, chances are they will not only return, but also tell others to come.

I relish my life here; I wrap it about me like a cocoon. This is what I know, and this is what I love. We still have faults, but withal, I am damn proud to call Mississippi home.

Norma Watkins

Norma Latimer Watkins was born at Baptist Hospital in Jackson, Mississippi, and attended Power and Duling Elementary Schools, Bailey Junior High, and Central High School. She was christened, confirmed, and married by Dr. Selah at Galloway Memorial United Methodist Church. She had four children at St. Dominic Hospital and graduated with honors from Millsaps College. And then she left.

For me, coming home to Mississippi was never easy. "You were notorious," my cousin Thomas Naylor said. If you flee the place where you were born, leaving a husband and four children behind, you *are* notorious, no matter how good your reasons for going might be. I left to escape bigotry and to go to graduate school, but I drove off with a civil rights lawyer and my departure was so thoroughly mingled with lust, every reason became suspect.

My father had a stroke and I began returning to Mississippi more often to visit him. On one of those trips I read in the paper that Eudora Welty would be celebrating her birthday with a public reception at Lemuria, a bookstore in Jackson. I decided to go.

Miss Welty and I had a history. At twenty-seven, I wanted to go back to college and signed up for classes at Millsaps. My father said, "You're a little old for this, aren't you?" I was, but I didn't care. With three children under six, my brain was turning to mush.

In high school I wouldn't have dreamed of going to my hometown Methodist college, where we heard they didn't allow makeup or dancing. Millsaps turned out to be nothing like that; it was a true community of learning and my world cracked open. I studied Emily Dickinson and wrote poetry. Poetry poured out of me as if someone had opened a vein. "Slow down," James Whitehead, my English professor said. I couldn't slow down; I was too far behind. I published my bad poetry in the school literary magazine; I sat on a tall stool in the cafeteria and read it out loud; I was drunk on learning.

The school announced that Eudora Welty would teach a creative writing course. Mother made fun of the fact that she was an old maid. "Isn't it fortunate that she can write. She's so very unattractive." What on earth did that matter? Eudora Welty was one of the country's most beloved writers and we were lucky to get her. I rushed to sign up for the course.

She told the class that nobody could teach us to write, she didn't want to fool us about that, but that she would read what we wrote and be as helpful as she could. I was terrible. All beginning writers are terrible; but Miss Welty was kind, finding something to praise in our feeblest efforts. She had a grand sense of humor and was more open-minded than I expected, for she seemed quite old, almost my mother's age.

My first story was about a woman whose husband beat her. She came weeping and dripping blood to our back door. I've forgotten the point or maybe there wasn't one, and Eudora hated it. "But it happened," I said. "So what?" she said.

For a year we met twice a week, writing three stories each term. She taught us to begin with the particular. She told us to be good listeners and to watch for connections. She said to look for the gesture that carries the feeling and to see not only what's there, but the thing behind what's there.

I decided to be a writer. What could prevent it? Miss Welty gave me A's, the school magazine liked me, and I had a circle of admiring artistic friends.

There was one problem. It was 1964, and the civil rights movement had arrived full force in Jackson. The fairground was filled with people who'd been arrested for the crime of riding into town on integrated buses. They were being hauled on other buses to Parchman state prison. Black churches were bombed. "By the N.A.A.C.P.," Daddy claimed. "They do it themselves to get sympathy." We had terrible fights at the dinner table.

"Just think," I said. "In a few hundred years we'll all have caramel-colored skin and no pimples."

Daddy said, "Miscegenation caused the fall of the Roman Empire." He gave me a copy of *Race and Reason*, which purported to prove people of color were innately inferior. I said, "What happened to 'respect everyone'? How about that Sunday school song, 'Red and yellow, black and white/All are precious in His sight'?" Things had changed, the South was at war, and I had come down on the wrong side.

In 1966, I finished Millsaps. I wanted to go away to graduate school and was offered a fellowship at the University of Arkansas. "Don't be ridiculous," my husband said. "You have a family to think of."

I met a circle of civil rights lawyers, bright men fighting to change the South, the first men I'd known who didn't have drawls. Daddy said, "They only came down here to sleep with the colored women."

One man in particular attracted me. His name was Bruce Rogow. He was good-looking and clever, and treated me as if I had a brain. He was leaving for Miami and asked me to come with him. I graduated with honors in June and left in July, taking clothes, books, and my writing.

The University of Miami offered me a fellowship that fall and I needed a recommendation to teach as a graduate assistant. I wrote to Eudora Welty, hoping she would brag on me. My return address was the only one I dared use: General Delivery at the University. I was terrified my family would come and drag me home, which my mother threatened regularly: "I'm sending your Uncle Doug," she wrote.

I wanted Miss Welty's blessing. My letter to her is lost, but I remember the tone. I didn't admit how lonely I was or how horribly I missed my children. I made life sound grand. I told her I had run away and sent a copy of the novella I'd written in honors class, asking if she'd pass it along to her agent. I told her to say I had a good mind. I over-reached, forgetting how much Eudora cared about family. She lived in her parents' house; she'd cared for a beloved brother through his illness, and told us she only taught to earn enough money to keep her mother in the best nursing home.

Her typed response dated July 29, 1966, reached me a few days later.

> Dear Norma,
>
> Your letter took me by surprise and has saddened me—I hope you are working things out.
>
> As to what you wanted, I don't really know anything first-hand I could tell the gentleman about either what you'd be teaching or the way you'd teach it. About what I am familiar with, your writing, I thought you were an A student in an undergraduate class at Millsaps, but I've no idea what interest your work would have to the higher levels in the academic world—or to the world in general, which is something else. Your stories, like everything you do, have a pleasing energy and vitality about them, and a dash that, in the writing, may be a style some day—I'm not sure it is now.
>
> And you don't need me to tell you you have a good mind. As to whether or not you have that indescribable but essential spark, the imagination, feeling for human beings, the extra thing that sparks a person to make a serious writer with real stories to tell—I don't think I could predict, it's too important and I wouldn't dare. I do feel your work, while good and entertaining and not without ambition, is still not anything "new," and I don't detect the wild streak of true and undeniable originality, though this is not to say it isn't buried somewhere under the surface. If you weren't, as I thought, asking me what I thought of your writing on the after-graduation level, forget what I've said—I only offer the opinion for what it's worth. I don't claim and never did claim, as my class knew, to tell anybody how to write their stories, or even whether to write their stories, and I don't tell you that now either.
>
> I sent back your ms. to the General Delivery address (the most depressing item about the letter you sent). I read it such a while ago now that I'm clear only in my impression that it was

interesting, ambitious, and worth doing, but that some of the approach is perhaps a bit self-indulgent. I'm guilty of the same thing sometimes, so I know what it means and whereof I speak. I know you wrestled hard and long with it, and your own satisfaction to have brought it into form at last must be worth a lot and should be.

This letter is probably unsatisfactory to you, but you see if you ask people to be a party to what you call running away, it puts them in a spot if they like you. I do like you and wish you well.* Take care.

Sincerely,
Eudora

[She signed the letter in pencil, adding a line in ink across the bottom.]

*I could only write you what I thought was true.

I couldn't believe I'd been so cocky, asking a favor like that from somebody famous. I put Eudora's letter in a suitcase with all the other mail I got that first year, telling me what a terrible person I was, and I tried to forget it. I never read it again all the way through, but what I remembered was that Miss Welty said I didn't care enough about people to be a writer.

Periodically I would tell myself, well, of course you aren't a writer; you're too selfish; you don't care enough about people to be a writer. Hidden away in that suitcase, the letter grew enormous, like a curse for running away. Eudora was a world-renowned writer; if she said I wasn't good enough, I wasn't. Maybe if I'd stayed in Mississippi with my husband and children the way I should have, I would be a writer, but I hadn't. When I took the letter out to frame it, I saw that what Miss Welty had said was worse: my work was not new; she didn't detect "the wild streak of true and undeniable originality."

In April of 1989, there I was, back in Jackson and headed to Lemuria with a palpable sense of dread. A line snaked out the door, waiting to greet Miss Welty, who was seated inside, patiently accepting the praise of her fans. I waited, trying to think what to say. Since that 1966 letter, we had not corresponded. I was a full professor now; I'd earned a master's and PhD, but I leaned over Miss Welty with the trepidation that silly young woman of twenty years before should have had.

I stuttered through the names I had accumulated: "I was Norma Craig, Norma Rogow, I'm Norma Watkins now—you probably don't remember me."

The eyes behind her glasses were shrewd and amused. "I remember you."

That was it, but her tone—the amused disdain—said it all. I moved along, my face flaming. I was the bad child. I had been cast out of paradise and I couldn't come home.

William Jeanes

William Jeanes left Mississippi to become a navy officer, to work in New York, to live for a time in the Bahamas, and again to work in New York. For twenty-one years he was a resident of Grosse Pointe, Michigan, before retiring—sort of—to Pass Christian in 1999. Along the way he was editor-in-chief of *Car and Driver* and publisher of that magazine and *Road & Track*, a senior vice president at two major advertising agencies, a front-row spectator at the Hurricane Katrina Show, coauthor of the marketing book *Branding Iron*, a successful freelance writer (*Sports Illustrated, American Heritage, Playboy, Saturday Evening Post, Smithsonian Air & Space*), Millsaps College's 1992 alumnus of the year, and the 2005 writer-in-residence at Northwestern University. He is a life trustee of Millsaps College and a board member of the Eudora Welty Foundation. He lives in Ridgeland with his wife, Susan.

You should know that I am living in Mississippi because of a series of accidents and happenstance. My entire life has been guided by accidents and happenstance, so this does not feel unusual to me. But it's only fair to say that I am not here altogether by choice.

Beginning in 1960, I left Mississippi three times and came back three times. Whether that makes me fortunate or qualifies me as a slow learner, I'm not sure. But I'm here, and inertia being what it is at the age when most things I buy will last a lifetime, I'm likely to remain.

How do I feel about that? I'm not sure about that either. Which is not surprising to me; Mississippi, after and above all, does not lend itself to certainties.

There are those who pleasure themselves by recitations of the supposed virtues of Mississippi. Good food, great people, a gentle way of life, a generous spirit, and so on. These are people who apparently don't read the *Clarion-Ledger*, or who for other reasons choose to ignore our state's obesity and its crime rate, to say nothing of our unemployment and intramural hostility.

They are in the main right about the generosity of spirit, and that makes up for a lot. Life—and there's no reason Mississippi should differ—is forever a series of offsetting qualities, cherished values in opposition to each other, and confusing contrasts. Few places on earth better illustrate this than does Mississippi.

Begin with history. In his novel *Requiem for a Nun*, Faulkner wrote, "The past is never dead. It's not even past." Put that thought into Latin, and Mississippi could have a far more appropriate state motto than *Virtue et Armis*, which translates loosely to "By valor and arms."

Valor and arms are two reasons you better think twice before you steal somebody's pickup truck.

Then there's our state flag, born in 1894. We are the last state in the union which still incorporates the CSA battle flag into its own state banner. A 2001 referendum to change the flag by replacing the CSA combat standard with a field of twenty stars arranged in concentric circles produced the following results at the polls: for the change, 36 percent; against it, 64 percent.

If you believe in majority rule, a system fast falling into disuse in our nation, you have to say, "So be it." But you don't have to like it.

I didn't care at all for the proposed redesign, which was clunky in the extreme, but when more than a third of our voters are opposed to the existing design, you might want to think about things in more depth. And maybe remember that the Ku Klux Klan proudly adopted the Confederate flag as its colors.

No wonder that a substantial number of Mississippians, even though a minority, are not enamored of the state flag as it now stands.

Be that as it may, where does one stop in today's world of political correctness? Do we change the name of Confederate Avenue up at Ole Miss to Insurgency Street? The university has already killed off

Colonel Rebel and replaced him with the Toddy Bear, or whatever the thing's called. Commentary on this milestone can begin and end with a large decal I saw on a Chevy Silverado: "The Bear Sucks." Crude, perhaps, but clear.

I, for one, am content to see the battle flag wave over cemeteries, Civil War battle sites, and memorial parks. There, it honors brave souls who brought it glory, albeit in a losing effort. Elsewhere, it probably does more harm than good. I don't think that many of us have any real interest in honoring the sensibilities of the great-great-grandchildren of those who fought.

We as twenty-first-century Mississippians would be well served if we applied three words to the Civil War: get over it.

One more word about political correctness as it applies to the 1861–65 conflict. "Dixie" is one of the greatest, most stirring songs ever written. Its authorship is not clearly established, though Dan Emmett is most often given credit for writing the piece. What is known is that the Yankee author—or authors—came from Ohio. Equally certain is that "Dixie" was a favorite of President Lincoln, who had it played at political rallies and on the occasion of General Lee's surrender.

"Dixie" ought to be played, and often. To those, no matter how high-minded, who think otherwise, *you* get over it. Tap your foot and enjoy life for a few minutes.

One of my enduring memories of Mississippi is an evening in the Grove at Ole Miss, sometime in the 1990s. A pair of uniformed members of the university band were strolling among the late-stayers, taking requests. "Dixie" was the most requested tune, which was not surprising. What was surprising was that the large tuba player was black, and the trumpet player was white. They appeared to be having a hell of a good time.

You can see what I mean about us being a people of surprising contrasts.

Togetherness can take unexpected forms.

Nowhere are there more surprises in Mississippi than in the world of religion. My own religion consists of the Golden Rule and the vast majority of the Ten Commandments. Not that it's any of your business. Further, I have not been to an actual church service, excluding weddings and funerals, for probably forty years.

Organized religion frightens me. That said, I have a great many friends who draw considerable comfort from attending church, singing hymns, and enjoying the fellowship. I even have friends in the clergy, and we enjoy each other. I respect these friends' beliefs and activities, and I spare them my feelings on the subject.

How did I get this way? By reading history. Our world has wiped out more people in the name of religion than for any other reason with the possible exception of megalomania and the simple urge to dominate. If you doubt this, you aren't watching or reading the news.

Understand that I am not saying that any person or any individual church is intrinsically evil. That's just not a defensible viewpoint. When my wife and I observed firsthand the destruction of our neighborhood and home during Hurricane Katrina, we also saw that the first responders with meaningful material help were church groups.

A Mennonite who brought his own bulldozer to Pass Christian cleared a path to the street through our backyard. He agreed to take enough money for fuel but no more. If the day comes when I feel the need to get religion, I intend to look into his.

What seemed like every Baptist church in Mississippi got to the Gulf Coast with amazing rapidity, beaten only by military and emergency vehicles. They brought gallons of water, food, and lots of clothing. And they did it because they believed it was the right thing to do. Never in my own experience was Mississippi's generosity of spirit and graciousness of attitude displayed to better advantage.

The Baptists were not alone, of course. Many others, people and organizations with no formal religious association and no agenda beyond the urge to help, showed up and helped us all. But it was the church groups who not only got there quickly, but also stayed for weeks and sometimes months.

Given my experience during just one disaster, how on earth could I stoop to criticize religion in any way? Well, I'll tell you. It befuddles and, to a degree, irritates me when religious Mississippians run into the streets howling about such earth-shattering threats to modern society as liquor by the drink. Would they feel better if we had liquor by the drum?

These folks should listen to the now-legendary speech by Ole Miss law professor N. S. "Soggy" Sweat in which he decries, and then praises, whiskey. Professor Sweat's bipolar treatment of demon rum is a pure example of contrasting beliefs and values. Besides that, it is laugh-out-loud funny.

I can see a reason or two to dislike whiskey—the headaches, for one thing—but when right-minded religious crusaders are seen on TV attacking the Harry Potter books as the work of the devil, I am moved to say to friends in other parts of the country: "These people aren't really from Mississippi. That footage was filmed on a secret Hollywood soundstage by godless communists."

No discussion of religion in our state would be complete without a nod to that ding-dong-daddy from Dumas, Mississippi, the Reverend Don Wildmon. Human decency dictates that I mention his poor health, something I wish on no one. But his use of religion to attack gays and to justify rampant censorship just doesn't set well with me. He does, of course, deserve credit for alerting us to Mighty Mouse's endorsement of opium because the reverend saw the diminutive superhero sniff a flower in a cartoon.

I can, however, agree with Reverend Wildmon that Islam is out to get us. How do the reverend and I know this? Because the Koran and Imams keep telling us so. Me and Don. How's that for a contradiction?

Finally, on religion, a mention of sex education in the public schools. On any number of occasions, you've surely heard some outraged preacher shrieking, "We are spending taxpayer money teaching our children to have sex!" I've got news for you and the preacher: our children already know how to have sex; what we're spending money on is teaching them not to have babies when they're thirteen years old.

Here we are in Mississippi with the highest teen pregnancy rate since the rape of the Sabine women, plus one of the highest infant mortality rates in the country, and we actually have people who want nothing done to stop it? Please.

Religion is like warts; we all have some. I won't show you mine if you don't show me yours.

My next topic is closely related to religion and is as inseparable from the inner soul of Mississippi as are grits and deer hunting. I speak of football. We are one of the few states in the country, maybe on earth, where a municipal school bond issue has been floated for the purpose of building an atomic nonskid hypoallergenic football field. Or whatever they call the newest grass substitute. To one who grew up in Mississippi, this makes perfect sense.

I lived in Corinth for the first eleven of my years, and my first football memory is a bunch of old people standing up in the grandstand at a homecoming game for the Corinth High Warriors. People got all teary, and I never forgot it.

The Warriors had once been champions of the Little 10, but then they joined the Big 8 and spent the next God-knows-how-many years getting the mortal hell beaten out of them. I thought the Big 8 was the work of Satan until we moved to Jackson in 1949, and I learned about the Central High Tigers.

From that time until I graduated with the CHS class of 1955, the Tigers lost about a half-dozen games. Football became part of my identity. Millsaps College saved me from a lifetime of football fanaticism and the cost of a condo in Oxford. The Majors lost a clear majority of the games its brave but minuscule squad played during my time there. They have since become a conference powerhouse, and I am proud.

I became an Ole Miss fan mostly because the majority of my friends went to school there and because of the patriarch of the Manning family. When Archie wore the red and blue, how could you not be for Ole Miss? I learned that being an Ole Miss fan is a serious calling. Ole Miss fans do not think it amusing, following a loss, when you offer to hire a grief counselor for them.

Earlier I mentioned the Grove. Whatever excesses might be committed in the name of Ole Miss football and however many endless alibis we on the outside must endure, the Grove makes it all worth it. I spent a quarter-century in Michigan and even did one term of graduate school at the university. You cannot imagine the differences in the great American pastime of tailgating as practiced at Oxford and Ann Arbor.

Participants in tailgating at Michigan dress as if they are on their way to a Third World garage sale. The average man and woman at a Mississippi deer camp dress better. In the Grove, grace and gentility hold sway with a determined elegance. The men dress less well these days, most of them wearing red Old Miss golf shirts stretched to the splitting point. The beautiful women are quite another matter; you fully expect to see that lovely O'Hara girl letting Charles Hamilton bring her dessert.

It bothers me that the Ole Miss football spending is about $9.5 million annually (Mississippi State spends nearly $13 million) in a state that's long been hurting on the education front. But that's relative peanuts compared with Auburn and Alabama ($28 million and $26 million). We comfort ourselves by knowing that State and Ole Miss each take in $18 million in football revenue, so at least the programs are profitable.

That, presumably, permits us to overlook public schools soliciting donations for school supplies and teachers buying supplies themselves despite their low salaries. But the overlooking isn't always easy.

After I finished my active duty as a navy officer, I took several English courses at what was then called the University of Mississippi Extension in Jackson. I have been told that this may qualify me to become an actual Ole Miss alumnus. Were I younger and had time to wait for a prime tent spot in the Grove, I'd look into that. Perhaps I can sell my alumni rights for a mess of turnip greens.

And there you have it, a few thoughts on why Mississippi gives me a great deal to think about. It has also given me a great many friends, old and new, who will be fun to have around as I move into my dotage.

If you grew up in Mississippi and even halfway liked it, you never leave. A part of Mississippi goes where you go. I never believed that to be true of Utah or Indiana or Minnesota. That perpetual Mississippi presence does not come about because we have the best of everything, or because Mississippi is the most beautiful place on earth, or because our people are the smartest, the bravest, or the best looking. It may be because we're the strangest—in a good way—and the most interesting.

For better or for worse, mostly better, I am here and will stay.

Willie Morris

Willie Morris, a native of Yazoo City, Mississippi, graduated from the University of Texas and studied at Oxford University as a Rhodes Scholar. He was editor of *The Texas Observer*, and served as editor-in-chief of *Harper's Magazine* from 1967 to 1971. He authored sixteen books, including *The Courting of Marcus Dupree*, winner of the Christopher Medal, and *North Toward Home*, winner of the Houghton Mifflin Literary Fellowship. Morris died in August 1999.

My people settled and founded Mississippi—warriors and politicians and editors—and I was born and raised into it, growing up in a town, half delta and half hills, before the television culture and the new Dixie suburbia, absorbing mindlessly the brooding physical beauty of the land, going straight through all of school with the same white boys and girls. We were touched implicitly, even without knowing it, with the schizophrenia of race and imbued in the deep way in which feeling becomes stronger than thought with the tacit acceptance that Mississippi was different, with a more profound inwardness and impetuosity and a darker past not just than that of New York, or Ohio, or California, but of Arkansas, Tennessee, Alabama, and Louisiana, which were next door. This was a long time before anyone deigned to think that a southerner could be elected president of the United States with everything that this would imply—not only elected in large measure with southern votes but, four years later, turned out resoundingly with southern votes as well.

I went away to college in Texas, and in England, and ran a newspaper in Texas, and sojourned in California, and edited a national magazine in New York City and, having served my time in our cultural capital as many of us must, moved out to the eastern tip of Long Island to a village by the sea.

I did not know then that I was an exile, almost in the European sense. When I met a fellow Mississippian by chance, the exchange of tales about family and places, the stories about football or fishing or some long-vanished preacher were signs of a strange mutuality. I would meet black Mississippians in the North who were more similar to me in background and preferences than the Yankee WASPs I saw every day.

I often dwell on the homecomings I have made—the acutely physical sensations of returning from somewhere else to all those disparate places I have lived. To the town of my childhood—Yazoo—it was the precarious hills looming like a mountain range at the apex of that triangle known as the Mississippi Delta, the lights of the town twinkling down at night in a diaphanous fog. To the city of my college days—Austin—it was the twin eminences of the University Tower and the grand old state capitol awash in light from very far away. To the citadel of my young adulthood—Oxford University—it was the pallid sunlight catching all in filigree the spires and cupolas of that medieval city on the Thames. To the metropolis of my ambition it was the Manhattan skyline that seemed so forbidding yet was at once so compact and close at hand. To the village of my gentlest seclusion, on Long Island, it was the Shinnecock Canal opening onto that other world of shingled houses, flat potato fields and dunes, and the blue Atlantic breakers.

It was in the East that I grew to middle age. I cared for it, but it was not mine. I lived nearly twenty years there, watching all the while from afar as my home suffered its agonies, loving and hating it across the distance, returning constantly on visits or assignments. The funerals kept apace, "Abide with Me" reverberating from the pipe organs of the churches, until one day I awoke to the comprehension that all my people were gone. As if in a dream, where every gesture is attenuated, it grew upon me that a man had best be coming on back to where his strongest feelings lay.

An acquaintance in Yazoo County writes me of the Big Black Swamp, where he has just been deer hunting. "I felt in a sacred spot," he says, "a kinship not only with my forebears, but with the land." His father and his uncle hunted there. So did his grandfather and great-grandfather and great-great-grandfather, the latter having come down here in the 1830s after the Choctaws had ceded their claim to the settlers. Now the Big Black woods are owned by big paper companies that lease out hunting rights. "Big Black Swamp has always been there," he laments, "a fixture, like the moon in the sky. When the paper companies feel they must 'harvest' their 'wood crop' there, will it become Big Black Parking Lot?"

The dilapidated shacks and the unpainted facades still abound, and although the paved streets and public housing in the older black sections of the towns seem prolific in contrast to the 1940s, a random drive through the rural areas or the larger cities reveals much of that same abject impoverishment, mainly black but white as well. Out in the delta, the very land itself seems bereaved with the countless half-collapsed, abandoned tenant shacks set against the copious delta horizon. These are testimonials to the largest mass exodus of a people in our history—the southern black migration northward since World War II. The triumph of Allis-Chalmers is everywhere, and the farm machinery companies pervade the landscape in such numbers as to astound one who remembers the numberless black silhouettes in these fields a generation ago, picking or chopping, pausing every so often to wave at the occasional car speeding by.

It is the proximity of Oxford and the Ole Miss campus, each populated by about ten thousand souls, that has given my homecoming its poignancy, for both have resonances of an older past. Youth and age are in healthy proportion, and the loyalty of the town to the university is both exuberant and touching. The courthouse in the middle of the square and the Lyceum at the crest of the wooded grove are little more than a mile apart, which is appropriate, for it is impossible to imagine Ole Miss in a big city, and Oxford without the campus would be another struggling northeast Mississippi town. One can drive around the campus and absorb the palpable sophistication of a small southern state university, and then proceed two or three miles into a countryside that is authentic boondocks upon which the twentieth century has only obliquely intruded.

Shortly after I came here, I was sitting on a sofa with Miss Louise, William Faulkner's sister-in-law. We were discussing the histories of some of the people buried in the cemetery. "It's an interesting town," she said. I told Miss Louise that I agreed. "It's so interesting," I replied, "I think somebody ought to write about it."

The presence of William Faulkner, the poet and chronicler of Mississippi, pervades this place, and living here has helped me know him better. His courage was of the Mississippi kind, and as with all great artists, he was a prophet on his own soil—about whites and blacks and the destruction of the land and the American century and the human heart. W. H. Auden wrote on the death of William Butler Yeats, "Mad Ireland drove him to poetry," and Mississippi worked this way on Mr. Bill, for something moved in him when he finally decided to come back and write about the people and things he knew the best, creating his mythical land out of the real fibers of everything around him. Yet at the time he was laboring in solitude on much of the finest work an American ever wrote, he was deeply in debt, Ole Miss had little or nothing to do with him, and the town was baffled and perplexed by him. To many he was a failed and drunken eccentric.

Racism has everlastingly been Mississippi's albatross, of course, and in coming home the native son could no more dwell upon his state without its racial background than he could change the color of his eyes. In these years we are seeing a Mississippi that is catching up to the social ideals and values of the older America—the one before Watts or Boston or Detroit, the one of the era when the eastern liberals considered themselves the black southerners' best friends before the black southerners arrived in such numbers, to find their allies had moved away to Westchester County.

Nowhere has all this been more evident than in the massive integration of the Mississippi public schools, an event that took place only ten years ago. This has brought dislocations, considerable local controversy over aptitude tests and class groupings, and a drift to private academies in many of the populous black counties. Yet who a generation ago would have dared predict the day-to-day manifestations of this profound change? It is still so very early, but the emerging biracialism of Mississippi can be seen everywhere—in the newspapers, television, parent-teacher meetings, sports events; in the friendships white and black youngsters have developed in the schools; in a politeness between the races in public places.

Earlier I tried to describe the acutely physical sensations of my returning in the past to all those disparate places I have lived. When I come back now to Oxford, Mississippi, my homecoming seems somehow to bring together the shattered fragments of all those old comings and goings.

Driving up Highway 7 past the little lost hardscrabble towns and the rough exteriors of an isolated America that has been forgotten, I sight the water towers of Ole Miss and the town silhouetted on the horizon, and then the lights of the square and Mr. Bill's courthouse, and the loops and groves of the campus with the Lyceum at the top of the hill, and the dark stadium in the distance. All of it seems to have sprung from the hard red earth for me, as the dispirited Roman legionnaire must have felt on reentering his outpost, his nexus of civilization, after foraging the forlorn stretches of Gaul.

"The writer's vocation," Flaubert wrote, "is perhaps comparable to love of one's native land." If it is true that a writer's world is shaped by the experience of childhood and adolescence, then returning at long last to the scenes of those experiences, remembering them anew and living among their changing heartbeats, gives him, as my writer friend Marshall Frady said, the primary pulses and shocks he cannot afford to lose. I have never denied the poverty, the smugness, the cruelty that have existed in my native state. Meanness is everywhere, but here the meanness, and the nobility, have for me their own dramatic edge, for the fools are *my* fools, and the heroes are mine too.

Yet, finally, when a writer knows home in his heart, his heart must remain subtly apart from it. He must always be a stranger to the place he loves, and its people. His claim to his home is deep, but there are too many ghosts. He must absorb without being absorbed. When he understands, as few others do, something of his home in America—Mississippi—that is funny, or sad, or tragic, or cruel, or beautiful, or true, he knows he must do so as a stranger.

Cynthia Walker

Cynthia Walker is a poetry and fiction writer who lives in peace and harmony in the woods of Jones County with her husband, screenwriter David Sheffield, and a plethora of animals. She has been a student, teacher, and publisher of literature and language, and considers her greatest gifts in life to be her meager talent as a horse whisperer and the time she now has with her remarkable parents, Marguerite and Guy.

W*e are living under the H in a bungalow that once belonged to 1930s chanteuse Ruth Etting, friend of gangster Bugsy Siegel, who lived more under the O or maybe even between the O and the first L. We are wishing for rain to dance on our new tin roof like Tennessee's cat. Irony grows on trees in Hollywood. It falls to the ground like the ripened citrus fruit in our backyard. We have snow dogs in a place where it never snows. We have to pay out-of-state tuition to send Morrison to Ole Miss. And most of our friends here are southerners. Palm trees understand irony. They, like us, are transplants.*

> *My mother lives in her own mother's house,*
> *And I wonder if one day I will live there too . . .*

This is the first line of a poem I wrote in 1979 as my flight to New York ascended into the autumn sky over New Orleans. The poem goes on to talk about the pets buried in Mamaw's backyard on 8th Avenue in Laurel, Mississippi, and how I can still remember the texture of St.

Augustine grass on bare feet, and the old brick street where we rode our bikes. It is the house where I have spent every Christmas of my life.

My Yankee grandparents moved to Laurel in 1920 and carved out a life on twenty thousand acres of piney wilderness, after having lived in New York, wearing opera capes and top hats and taking cruises to Europe. The place they built "out in the country" was the three-story log house where my father grew up, and, many years later, where I grew up riding horses and herding cattle. They called it Reklaw Ranch, the family name spelled backwards.

As an adolescent, I explored the attic full of treasures from a life that seemed a million miles and centuries away. I dressed in my grandmother's satin gowns and studied the watercolors of the Hudson River Valley artists my grandfather had collected. I read their books on Chinese mythology, the American and English classics, first edition poetry books and novels, and diaries and journals from their travels.

The log house at Reklaw burned to the ground the year after my husband, David Sheffield, and I left for New York. Most of the land was eventually sold, except for a small section on Tiger Creek in Ovett that would one day play an important role in our return to the South. But those were not our thoughts at the time. We were grown up-baby boomers, a high school French teacher and an aspiring writer from Biloxi, and we didn't think a lot about the distant future, only the present, and as soon as we could find a decent apartment in Manhattan, the world would be ours.

The most frequently asked question of a southerner in New York in those days was, "How did you get here from *there?*" You wanted to say *barefoot in the back of a chicken truck,* but instead you told your story, which in our case was a journey straight out of Joseph Campbell: first comes the call to the lowly hero to leave his home and go on a quest. Our call came from actor friend Patrick who was auditioning at *Saturday Night Live:* "*Hey, Dave, they like your stuff up here, some producer guy, he's tall and wears glasses. . . . Oh, gotta go, they're puttin' out cheese in the green room.*"

From that cryptic call, David was hired as a writer for *Saturday Night Live.* Our friend Cindy said, "Okay, you're gonna go there, make some money, and then come home, right?" And that was the plan. David and his new partner Barry Blaustein wrote some of the most memorable sketches of the show, like "Gumby," "Buckwheat," "James Brown's Celebrity Hot Tub Party," and "Mr. Robinson's Neighborhood." Our son, who was thirteen at the time, has a photograph of a grinning Eddie Murphy signed, *"To Morrison . . . can you say bitch?"*

Life in New York was an urban adventure. I walked the entire city, exploring with my brother, Wendell Walker, as my companion and guide. Wendell became a New Yorker the day after graduation and I assume he will always be one. He is now a director at Museum of the Moving Image in Astoria. We stayed in New York for three years, but there were more dragons to slay, and, according to Joseph Campbell, we had to meet an old crone who would show us the way. He arrived in the flamboyant person of John Gaines, David's first Hollywood agent, who felt it was time for "the boys" to go west and start writing movies.

The huskies are watching the horizon, waiting for the music of rain on tin. The Los Angeles weatherman, who never says much of anything, has predicted showers. The tin roof is supposed to remind us of home. Our walls are white and our peg-and-groove floors are painted silver, with dimes fitted into the peg holes. We imagine Ruth Etting dancing on these floors with her gangster boyfriend Moe the Gimp, and maybe even Bugsy Siegel with some Hollywood starlet.

One day Moe came home from Chicago and found Ruth in flagrante delicto with her piano player and shot him five times in what is now our bedroom. He lived; no ghost. We play a scratchy version of "Ten Cents a Dance," in honor of Ruth and our shiny new floors and we hang our new movie poster of Doris Day and James Cagney as Ruth and Moe in Love Me or Leave Me. *In other words, we have gone whole-hog Hollywood. Fourteen white, powder-coated chandeliers hang artistically grouped like grapes in the foyer; we have a red wagon full of bricks for a coffee table. All of our furniture is on wheels. David says maybe we can roll it all over to Beverly Hills. We are, after all, the new generation of Beverly Hillbillies.*

In 1985, I started a poetry journal called *Saturday Afternoon*. For fifteen years we published the cream of the new Hollywood poetry scene. In 1995, I wrote a play called *A Vampire in Hollywood* that had a successful run at Theater/Theatre in Hollywood. I wrote three television pilots and many screenplays, some of which were optioned, but Hollywood was David's testing ground. And he was passing with flying colors. *Coming to America* and *The Nutty Professor* were huge box office hits. I needed something of my own. I decided to bring Mardi Gras to Hollywood.

I was celebrating Fat Tuesday in New Orleans when my dad, who was once president of the American Paint Horse Association, called from Mississippi to say a new filly had been born. She was the last of his line of paints that once adorned the landscape at Reklaw like a quilt of sorrel, brown, buff, and white on the green pastures of sweet rye grass. On Ash Wednesday I met the filly, named her Mardi Gras, and made plans for her to be transported out to Hollywood as a yearling.

I had found my passion for the new century: I started rescuing horses. First I adopted Bugsy from the rental string at Sunset Ranch, home of the Hollywood Dolls Horse Club. I became a board member of the rescue group and rode Bugsy in the Hollywood Christmas Parade for the next three years. Bugsy was named, not for the gangster from my neighborhood, but for his big blue eyes. He and I bonded over many rides to the Hollywood sign, the Mexican Restaurant in Burbank, and the caves in Griffith Park. My friend Millicent rode Diablo, a rescued Appaloosa. Bugsy and Diablo were best friends, and sometimes when we rode at night, the fog was so thick we couldn't see each other, but the horses knew the way and were sure-footed. We galloped home over the winding paths up and down the hills, branches hanging low, canyons gaping on all sides, drops that would kill us all, but Bugsy would keep his nose on Diablo's white butt and we always made it home.

We are at Eddie Murphy's fortieth birthday party at a club in downtown Los Angeles. Lori Blaustein and I are dressed in ubiquitous black outfits, surrounded by colorful bling bra tops and low-riding skintight flare legs. In other words we are the only women on the dance floor not showing navel. Eddie's wife, Nicole, makes us feel at home, but we look like funeral directors, especially compared to her leggy model friends. Nicole is outrageously beautiful. On stage, Stevie Wonder is getting ready to sing "Happy Birthday" to Eddie. Of course he can't see that Eddie is not standing there.

Eddie is out back with our husbands, David and Barry, his writers. Some new project will come from this evening. Lori and I look at each other and wonder what to do. We look like security guards in our black outfits. We could say something. But Stevie Wonder is a professional. He just starts singing. Eddie makes it back before the end of the song, much to our relief. He always calls me Mrs. Sheffield. I say, "Happy birthday, Eddie." He says, "Hello, Mrs. Sheffield; you sound so country." I reply, "I am country, Mr. Murphy."

On Valentine's Day, 2003, Mardi Gras arrived at Sunset Ranch where we were settled in as boarders with three other horses. Mardi joined them in the stalls on the edge of a hill where we had a view of the city of Los Angeles. From here we watched the sunset while we relaxed at our umbrella table nestled among our herd, in the shadow of the O and the D. For a long time we thought, "How could it get any better than this?" But one day we looked at each other and that nagging feeling returned.

This is great, but it isn't ours. And it isn't home.

We became obsessed with the idea of owning our own horse farm, and the more we looked out west, the more we knew our paradise was waiting for us on the two hundred acres of pine forest my grandparents had clear-cut and replanted in 1920. When we sold our house on Lake Hollywood Drive and the baby grand left the building, I allowed myself the brief memory of Dudley Moore playing "As Time Goes By" one wild night in Hollywood.

I think that is the way of journeys. One day they just end.

I was a California girl. I was a New Yorker. *I am and always will be a southerner.*

> *My mother lives in her own mother's house*
> *And I wonder if one day I will live there too.*

The house on 8th Avenue will outlive us all. My eighty-eight-year-old mother plants pansies around the crepe myrtle trees the way Mamaw once did. My eighty-eight-year-old father and I talk on the phone every day. One of our favorite topics is how we have gone full circle bringing horses back to Reklaw. I love that my new life is a continuation of his passion. Perhaps we will breed Mardi and continue the line. My old horse, Bugsy, must put on weight if he is to make it through next winter. He grazes with eight-year-old Mardi and three other horses in a big pasture of Bermuda grass. Our old dog, Louis, the husky, some mornings chooses not to get up.

Wild turkeys roam the dam of our lake. Deer feed in our forest. There is plenty of rain on the tin roof. We are cultivating our garden like good students of Voltaire. I look back and wonder that it took so many dragons, oracles, and crones, all necessary to get me to this point, this grassy spot in the sun, this third act of my life.

When a wind blows across the lake and the horses gallop from the pasture to the barn with the promise of relief from the heat, I start thinking about Christmas. I am home. This is where Christmas lives. As for Hollywood and Manhattan, I visit. It was a great trip. We didn't bring home the grail, but there are some cases of fine California chardonnay.

Michael Farris Smith

Michael Farris Smith is a native Mississippian, and has spent time living in France and Switzerland. He is the author of the novella *The Hands of Strangers*, and his fiction and nonfiction have appeared in numerous literary reviews and anthologies. His new novel, *Rivers*, will be published by Simon & Schuster. He is the recipient of a Mississippi Arts Commission Literary Arts Fellowship and has twice been nominated for a Pushcart Prize. He lives in Columbus, Mississippi, with his wife and two daughters in their turn-of-the-century Victorian home.

A couple of weeks ago I was preparing to travel to Paris for about a week. As I walked into our living room my wife was sitting on the love seat. Spread across her lap and falling to the floor was our favorite family blanket. Like many things put to good use, the blanket has come unraveled over time, the patchwork splitting and small white bits of padding hanging out of the breaks in the pattern. On the floor next to the love seat was her sewing box. She was in the beginning stages of stitching the blanket, working patiently with a needle and white thread. Our baby had just been put to sleep in her crib, and our six-year-old was getting her evening dose of cartoons.

When I saw what she was doing, I had a strange sensation of pride in the fact that the blanket had survived this long, and that it is adored enough to be salvaged. I stood in the middle of our living room for a moment, a wife sitting on one side of the room, a daughter on the other, another daughter sleeping, baby toys and Barbie dolls and family photos the dominant decorative accessories, and I thought about this blanket and the journey I have taken with it.

The blanket was purchased on a cold, breezy day in Geneva, Switzerland. I had just moved into an apartment on Rue de Carouge, a street along the tram route and only a block over from the strong flowing river. I had little furniture, a few books, a random collection of plates and coffee cups and silverware, and no blanket. A dozen or more empty wine bottles were standing across my bedroom floor, candles sticking out of them, which I lit and used for extra warmth at night. I did have a bed, but only a set of sheets, and I wasn't going to sleep another winter's night without a blanket.

So I wrapped up and walked a couple of blocks to the grocery store, which had a small home accessory aisle, and fortunately, they had a blanket. A blanket, as in one, which I bought, hurried back to my apartment with, and slept happily under until the Geneva spring came along, and the clouds moved away from the Alps, and the snow melted and raised the river.

I obviously thought nothing about it at the time. It was just a blanket. I had plenty else to keep me occupied. I was in the third year of living abroad, mostly in Geneva, sometimes in Paris, sometimes in the hotel rooms of cities such as Rome, Madrid, London, Munich, Barcelona, Milan. I had dumb-lucked my way into a job that was not only taking me to these wonderful places, but paying me a salary to go. And I had not for one moment, since I had gotten on the plane in Jackson, and stepped off in Paris, regretted it. Honestly, I had no plans to return to the States. Ever. I had become a part of the lifestyle, inspired by the architecture and the history, at home in the cafes and quaint restaurants, comfortable in the discoveries I was making about myself and the world around me.

When I bought that blanket, I was unaware that my remaining time in Geneva was limited. Less than a year later, our company would move to Paris, and shortly after that, the payroll was trimmed and I found myself packing a giant bag that I would somehow manage to get to the Paris airport, and eight hours later my life abroad came to a painful end. In the following weeks, there was still some question as to whether I would ever return, but I already seemed to know that this part of my life was over. And I wasn't happy.

I had been so mad about it all; I pretty much sold everything not nailed down in my apartment for about one-twentieth of what it was worth. Bed, coffee table, sofa, love seat, bookshelves, kitchen table, dinner table and chairs. It was all unloaded at beneath bargain prices. I watched as happy buyers walked out with uniquely crafted furniture pieces that I had gradually accumulated at the Saturday market at Plainpalais, a park in the center of Geneva. Pieces of furniture I myself had bargained for, wrestled onto a tram, wrestled up four flights of a skinny staircase because they wouldn't fit into a skinny elevator. It didn't feel like it was only pieces of furniture I was getting rid of, but pieces of Geneva. Pieces of my life there, that I had loved.

For some reason, when it came time to pack my clothes and other keepsakes, I packed up the blanket and stuck it in that giant bag with everything else.

Thirteen years later, on the eve of a visit to Paris, a place that has been such an inspiration to me as both a person and as a writer, I stood in the living room of my home, watching my wife handle the blanket with a delicate touch, working to keep it a part of our lives. A part of my life. And I wondered what that blanket would have said to me back then, if it could have spoken, as I stomped around my apartment, as I stared out of my fourth-floor window, as I dropped my head a little more as the day of my departure drew closer.

I bet it would have said, "You're going home. You have come here and you are different now, but not wholly different, just blended with what you were before. You were Mississippi, a little-league field in Magnolia, the Pike County back roads, the hay barn at your grandfather's place. You were the gospel choirs on Sunday morning, homemade ice cream and cold watermelon, the spring-fed river that was cold in July. You were people praying when things got tough, lightning bugs and honeysuckle, the sound of the passing train easing you to sleep at night. You were all those things. And you still are. You are now those things, and something else. But you are going home. And one day I will keep your wife warm, and one day your daughters will crawl across me on your living room floor, and one day we will have shared so much together, I will need to be stitched."

I went to Paris. Walked the streets that I adore. Stopped at old haunts, looked for the ghosts. I dreamed of new stories. Remembered the old ones.

And when it was time to leave, I was ready to come home to Mississippi.

Wyatt Cooper

Wyatt Cooper was born on a farm in Quitman, Mississippi, in 1927, graduated from high school in New Orleans, and attended the University of California–Berkeley and U.C.L.A., where he majored in theatre arts. He was an actor on stage and in television, a screenwriter, and an editor. He was married to the artist Gloria Vanderbilt, and they lived in New York with their two sons, Carter and Anderson, who is now a CNN news correspondent.

Going Home

O dream of joy! Is this indeed
The Lighthouse top I see?
Is this the hill? Is this the kirk?
Is this mine own countree?
                    —Coleridge

My heart's in the Highlands, my heart is not here;
My heart's in the Highlands, a-chasing the deer;
A-chasing the wild deer, and following the roe—
My heart's in the Highlands wherever I go.
                    —Robert Burns

Thomas Wolfe wrote a book and called it *You Can't Go Home Again.* That is a catchy title and it caught on. It caught on with people, even, who know nothing of the great autobiographical novel that went with it. One often hears it quoted, repeated with the half-jocular, half-embarrassed shrug that accompanies axioms from the Bible, Shakespeare, or *Poor Richard's Almanac*. As is usual with such popular utterances, it caught on precisely because it is part profound truth and part arrant nonsense.

We recognize the truth of it because each of us has at one time or another undertaken that almost mythical journey back to the familiar landscape that used to be home, to confront, instead, a land that is foreign and unfamiliar. That this is so is, of course, not the fault of the place. A place, after all, is only trees, ground, water, soil, and the uses men have put them to. We must credit it, instead, to the heavy burden we lay upon the trip. We go encumbered by an unreasonable demand, unspoken and not even totally formed, that in some mysterious way the questions of a lifetime should be answered there, the hungers of a lifetime assuaged. We hope, perhaps, that we will be able to reach back in time and correct something in our shaping that needs correcting. I dream from time to time that I am making improvements on the house I grew up in, though this house has not existed for ten years. We take with us a troubling sense of longing and of loss. We travel with a haunting mixture of memory and desire. We set out on the nostalgic road with the hope and faith and expectation of the child that once was, with that child's tenderness and innocence, which are not only not what they were but perhaps never even existed as they are recalled, and which are, in fact, an adult's poignant, reconstructed, partly calculated, and carefully nurtured idea of what he himself has been.

He expects to see the giants of his childhood and to know once more those towering and superhuman parents and teachers, neighbors and friends who gave form and shape to his youth, who seemed to move in a world of assurance and competence, and whose eyes were the mirrors in which he first formed images of himself. He expects or hopes to find them not the ordinary mortals they are, with limited knowledge, primitive notions, and narrow interests, complaining about the rising cost of meat and boasting about the town's recent erection of a power plant, but the concerned, judicious, all-knowing authorities he remembers, who once gave him answers and quieted his fears.

He expects to find intact and unchanged the church and the school that helped to mold him, which were so much more than wood and stone and once seemed absolute and everlasting and immovable, guardians of all the certainty in the world, where the depth and breadth of his thoughts, feelings, and impulses were first plumbed.

He finds that they have vanished. If they are physically there, unchanged even, they have become somehow shrunken, diminished, flat, and devoid of any life he recognizes, peopled by strangers of a smaller and lesser race, a company now of dwarfs whose comings and goings have nothing of the burning passions, swelling ambitions, consuming thoughts, raging fears, strange intensities, compelling laughter, or vexing tears that he remembered in them and in himself.

And he expects to come upon himself: to see the towheaded youth, all eager eyes and lengthening bones, with fair freckled skin under a frayed straw hat, barefoot and in overalls, climbing the red clay hill with the distracted air of the born daydreamer, the pale, lonely prince somehow disguised as the farmer's son.

But he is not there. Instead, there are ghosts, glimpses, and hints that tease and tantalize. When he was not looking, life went on. Faces, minds, bodies have altered. The very look of the land has changed. Where once there were hills, there is flat land. It is all gone, washed away by a thousand rains. During the decades it has flowed across the fields, along the ditches, and down the little river, on to bigger rivers, and eventually out to the great uncaring sea. It seems so simple but so unlikely that so much could flow so surely away on such a little stream, that little stream with the Indian name that sits now, hardly moving, evaporating under a hot summer sun.

But so it is, and, instead, he comes upon himself as a middle-aged man with a tiring body, a declining spirit; he is thrown back upon the person he has become.

He sees people. He is hailed by those he knew. He is recognized and remembered. His hand is shaken and his back is slapped, and he in his turn shakes hands and slaps backs. Smiles and hearty remarks are exchanged, but they know nothing of what the years have been for him, little of his dreams for himself or of his place in the world. As he knows nothing of them and of theirs. Together they recall the past; they compare dates and occurrences; they shake their heads over those who have died or been ruined; they smile with pride over children who have become doctors or salesmen or computer scientists or housewives or mothers, and they joke about the improbable presence of a generation of grandchildren. Photographs are displayed. Cheerfully they deny in each other the evidence of graying or vanishing hair and withering flesh. Then they go their separate ways, making promises that will not be kept, wearing a glow that will last for a little, relishing for a time the tender residue of that reaching out, that tentative touching of another familiar life, cherishing the moments of sweet reunion with someone who is not quite a stranger, someone with whom there is something of a shared past, but afterward feeling more lonely, more alone, and more mortal, feeling somehow disturbed, somehow at a loss, somehow less enlightened, and altogether more puzzled about the meaning in it all.

That much, then, of Thomas Wolfe's title is true. But in another sense there is foolishness in it because, as no one knew better than Thomas Wolfe, we go home in our thoughts all the time, sometimes when we have no idea we are doing it. We have in truth never left home, for we carry it around with us. It is a part of our dreaming and our waking. It is a part of our breathing. It is a part of all we have been, all we are, and all we shall ever be. I doubt that there is a day in my life in which some fleeting image of that treasured country does not cross my inner eye. I will suddenly become aware that I have been standing beside the path that led down to the pump behind the schoolhouse, or I will for a moment see clearly the two giant hickory trees beside the road to Grandma's. I will remember the pervading smell of new overalls on the first day of school or the act of lighting the kerosene lamps in the kitchen and the comforting aroma of the biscuits a busy mother made for our supper. I remember driving the cows home from the pasture in the late afternoons, under the red sky of sunset, moving slowly and lazily, striking with my stick at weeds along the path, dreaming hazy dreams of glory, watching out for snakes and stinging nettles, avoiding the cows' droppings. I can close my eyes and know once more the lurking sense of terror as twilight faded and darkness gathered in clumps at the edge of the woods. I can hear the wail of the congregation singing at night in the church nearby, the collective sound of it floating mournfully through the still mystery of a starlit world, riding on the air with the scent of honeysuckle or crabapple bloom, and mingling in my ear with the cries of crickets, of frogs, of whippoorwills, and the rhythmic creaking of the porch swing I sat in. I recall the novelty of an airplane passing overhead and my sister Janice, who had never seen one on the ground, speaking both our thoughts when she said, "I don't want a plane to fall, but if one is going to fall, I wish it would fall near here so we could see it."

Sometimes walking and talking with my sons, I will hear in my own voice the voice of my father echoing from all those years ago, and I will know once again the strange fascination his mysterious presence held for me. I hear his rich voice vibrate against the trees we move among, and in it I can now hear something of pain, something lost and lonely, I was then too young to recognize or suspect in others.

I remember the sights and sounds and smells of home because the memory of home is the thing that never leaves us.

There is a familiar old saying, "You can take the boy out of the country but you can't take the country out of the boy," and, whatever your country has been, however alien it may have seemed to you at the time, or however alien to it you may have felt, it is forever a part of what you are, what you become, and what you mourn for.

And the core of it, the center around which all revolves, is the family: the father that was, the mother that was, the brothers and sisters, the uncles, aunts, grandparents, friends and neighbors—all exist forever in some part of what you are and what you do. They are as inescapable as life, as inevitable as death, and even if you somehow shut them out of your waking mind, they remain a part of everything that moves, molds, and renews you. You live with them and they with you.

Judy H. Tucker

Judy H. Tucker, an independent editor and playwright, was awarded a Literary Arts Fellowship by the Mississippi Arts Commission in 2007. Her plays have been produced and/or read at New Stage Theater and Fondren Workshop Theatre in Jackson, the Alabama Shakespeare Festival, and the University of Southern California, Los Angeles. Tucker has compiled and coedited a series of eight anthologies with Charline R. McCord. In addition, she has also collaborated with Lottie Boggan on three short story collections.

W hen I told my father I was getting married, he said to me, "Well, if you marry an engineer, you'll always be moving. They follow the work." Daddy was right. I relished the idea of new places but I wasn't giving up my home. From the earliest days of our state when the Choctaws were resettled to the Oklahoma Territory, my father's family has lived on the same farm in a small community in Leake County called Hopoki or Hopoca, a Choctaw word meaning something akin to "far away."

I felt safe on the farm. The land furnished all our needs, from the timber in our houses to the "cash crop" of cotton, to the barnyard and the garden and orchards. I knew every acre of the place, where every plum tree grew, the huckleberry thickets, the pink honeysuckle, dogwood, the purple violets, the rooster heads. I loved every inch of the land, and still do, but as the sixties approached, I began to understand that some folk were not so lucky as I.

When the years of the civil rights movement came upon us, I knew instantly which side I was on. Why had I never questioned this racial divide before? Simply because it had never occurred to me. I lived in the kingdom of Hopoki, a very real world and an imaginary fairy tale. We owned the world as I knew it, and there was no strife in this world.

Just as the "troubles" grew worse and argument and angry words flew all around the South, my engineer husband took me away. We always lived in the state capitals, and finally we moved to our nation's capital and that was best of all. We saw the cherry blossoms bloom, we could take a train to the Big Apple and return the very same day. All these delights were close: the Smithsonian, the National Gallery, Lord & Taylor down the road, Tanglewood nearby.

I learned what I call my "social skills," tennis and bridge, and they proved their value. The children walked to school, and every family in our neighborhood was new to the area, so there was no social status to contend with. On the downside, we were more aware of the "troubles." We read a story in the *Washington Post* that was different from what we'd read in the local paper back home. I had to try to explain my home state at every turn. Once I was at a party on Capitol Hill when someone asked me, "Where are you from?" When I said Mississippi, they stared at me and said, "What are you doing here?"

When we'd had enough of the moving van, we packed up one last time and returned to Jackson, close enough to the farm to be home. On our first trip back to the farm, we couldn't find it! Was it a fairy tale after all? No, the county had changed the route of the road. We soon learned to appreciate the asphalt.

But the best change, the most gratifying change, was to see blacks and whites going to school together, working side by side at businesses, eating meals at the same table.

And there was now plumbing inside the old farmhouse.

Scott Stricklin

Scott Stricklin, Mississippi State University athletic director, was born in Jackson, Mississippi, and is a 1992 graduate of MSU, where he volunteered as a freshman in the athletic department information office. After graduation, he worked in MSU's athletic program, which led him to Auburn, Tulane, Baylor, University of Kentucky, and then back to MSU. He and his wife, Anne, have two daughters, Abby and Sophie.

Like many Mississippians, I was born with a love of sports. Neither of my parents was passionate about sports, though my mother displayed a passing interest. But my older brother and I were always playing, watching, or talking about games.

Neighborhood football games often took place in our wide front yard. Since most of the players were closer to my brother's age—he is five years older—the games involved tackling. I always thought my very participation in these games was a badge of honor. The games were physical, but they began to teach me important lessons that all Mississippians learn eventually: lessons about hard work, dedication, passion, and fun.

Much to my father's chagrin, his lush manicured lawn always suffered from the wear and tear of these contests. Each fall, as bare patches developed where grass once stood, my dad would complain and implore us to find another location for our football games. But Mom would always end the conversation by saying, "The grass will come back and will always be here. Our boys won't."

Just as they are today, fall weekends were a special time for a football fan in Mississippi's capital city. On Saturdays, I'd turn on the radio or TV to follow SEC football. This was during the 1980s, when Mississippi State and Ole Miss regularly played games in Jackson at Mississippi Veterans Memorial Stadium, and the highlight of the season was convincing my parents to take us to see real, live college football games.

Sundays always began with church, followed by a mad dash home to watch the then-hapless New Orleans Saints on TV. I'm too young to remember Archie Manning in college, but I remember him starring for the Saints, and I decided early on that my chosen profession would be NFL quarterback. When my fifth-grade football coach decided I was an offensive lineman rather than a quarterback, my goals shifted. Rather than running the Saints' offense when I became an adult, I would instead run the whole team by buying the franchise.

Sometime during my junior high and high school years, the dream of buying the New Orleans Saints settled into a desire to work in athletics. And not just athletics, but college athletics.

And so, on the first day of my freshman year at Mississippi State, I volunteered to work in the athletic department's sports information office. Suddenly, access to a full spectrum of Southeastern Conference athletic events lay before me. Working football, basketball, and baseball games became my routine. During that freshman year, I volunteered at the SEC Men's Basketball Tournament in Knoxville (fitting, since that is the home of the Volunteers), and I came to another realization: if I worked hard and had a degree and made enough positive impressions on enough people, then someone might one day hire me to actually work in athletics.

Soon enough, despite more hours spent in the press box than in the classroom, I had the degree. An entry-level job at State led to another entry-level job at Auburn, which is where I found my new bride, Anne, and where I would remain for a couple of years before returning to our home state for good.

Those "couple" of years became five years in east Alabama, then a year in New Orleans (Tulane), four more in Central Texas (Baylor), followed by five years in the bluegrass (Kentucky). Each stop allowed us to make new friends and create wonderful memories, but also brought a reminder that home was still Mississippi.

With my parents in Jackson and my wife's parents in Starkville, Anne and I had built-in reasons to return to Mississippi a couple of times each year. These visits allowed us to see old friends, eat at our favorite Mississippi restaurants, and watch our state's progress over time.

When our daughters were born—one in Texas and the other in Kentucky—the trips back to the Magnolia State became orientation sessions for these newest Stricklins, allowing them to see where their parents grew up and learned about life.

The opportunity to return to Mississippi came in an unexpected way. My good friend Greg Byrne and I had worked together at Kentucky. Greg's dad, Bill, was a longtime athletic director at Oregon, Nebraska, and Texas A&M, and Greg had grown up around the world of college athletics.

One day in 2005, Greg pulled me into his office at UK to tell me he was getting out of athletics. He said it was time for him to see if he could enjoy working in the "real world." I think we both knew what the answer would be, and the very next year Greg decided to get back into athletics. And he did, taking a job at Mississippi State.

Two years later, Greg was promoted to athletic director and called to offer me the chance to return home and work for him. Life is funny; a guy from Oregon brought me back to Mississippi.

Two years later, after Greg returned to his West Coast roots by taking the AD job at Arizona, I got the same promotion Greg had received a couple of years earlier.

I didn't end up buying the Saints, but being athletic director at an SEC school—at my alma mater—is a pretty fair alternative. And much cheaper.

There are times when I sit back and reflect on my journey—on my time growing up in Jackson, my college years as a student worker in the athletic department, our fifteen-year odyssey across the southern United States. Those reflections lead me to the friends I made, the memories we shared, and the places I temporarily called home. But most of all, the reflections make me think of the lessons I first learned playing tackle football in my parents' front yard, the ones about hard work, dedication, passion, and fun.

One lesson learned is that you don't have to leave Mississippi to follow your dreams. There are plenty of opportunities for young people in our beloved state. But if you do leave, you can always return.

Today, my father's lawn is green and lush, with no discernible bare spots. The grass came back, and so did his sons, raising their families in Mississippi, just as he did.

Carolyn Haines

Carolyn Haines grew up in Lucedale, the daughter of newspaper own-ers/journalists. She joined the family business as a journalist, and af-ter ten years switched to fiction writing. She is the recipient of many awards for her fiction, the latest being the 2011 RT Reviewers' Choice Award for her mysteries, the 2010 Harper Lee Award for Distinguished Writing, the 2009 Richard Wright Award for Literary Excellence, and a writing fellowship from the Alabama State Council on the Arts. She has published more than sixty books in a number of genres. She is an avid animal rights activist and an assistant professor of English at the University of South Alabama, where she teaches the graduate and undergraduate fiction classes. For more information on Haines and her work, go to www.carolynhaines.com.

Home is such a powerful concept, especially for a writer. In a world where many people have come to view their "homes" as investments— a thing to be sold for a profit, some temporary place like a Motel 6—I am a homebody. My home is my refuge and my castle, though it is most ordinary to the gaze of others.

Most of my days are spent on my small farm in Semmes, Alabama, with my abundance of stray animals and my solitary hours of imagina-tion and writing. When I leave the farm, it is usually to promote my latest book or to go to the university to teach a class. It's an amusing fact to many people that I live only about thirty-five miles from the place where I grew up—Lucedale, Mississippi.

The border between the two states, along what used to be called

Bloody 98, is the Escatawpa River, an amber body of water with pure white sandbars. I learned to swim there with my mother and brothers. When I was growing up, the river wasn't considered a boundary line; it was a place to play. We sank watermelons in the clear, cold water or hand-cranked homemade ice cream on the riverbank. My childhood is filled with memories of the small farms and pine forests around George County and the sidewalks of small-town Mississippi.

I'm physically very close to my hometown—and I wasn't one of the popular kids—so what then is this desire to live once again within the boundaries of a state with such a troubled past? I can only tell you that I long to go home.

Perhaps the "home" to which I want to return is more in the vein of Dorothy and her desire to get back to Auntie Em and a Kansas that was a place of safety. I want to click my heels and return to the summer of 1960, to the place where I picked peas with Joe Vesely, the police chief of Lucedale and an honest and honorable man. A place where doctors came to my home at midnight and sat with my sick grand- mother and held her hand until she felt better. A place where we slid on cardboard boxes down the pine-straw laden front lawn of Neal's Hill at the end of Ratliff Street. And a place where my mother sent hot lunches each day to Miss Hattie and Miss Mattie, elderly sisters who lived two houses down from us.

Home was a place where I could ride my horse for hours on end down narrow dirt lanes in the Bexley and Merrill communities and stop for water at a stranger's house and be welcomed.

Perhaps it is the past that I hunger for more than any particular place. All I know is that Mississippi—the best of Mississippi—has been lodged in my brain as this sun-drenched rural locale that I have now sought for the last thirty years. It is a place of dirt roads that lead through pine timber and hardwood groves. There are streams just wide enough for my horse to jump and clean enough that I can take a cool sip. Mississippi is populated with neighbors who come out to their front gate to greet a passerby and ask after my grandmother and family.

In the Mississippi of my mind, people still live close enough to the land to know that horses are flight animals. A car speeding past, churning gravel and blaring a horn, may show the driver's irritation at the horrible inconvenience of being delayed a few moments—but even if impatient, those phantom drivers from the past behaved with courtesy. In my Mississippi, folks don't mind a tiny delay to keep a neighbor safe.

There are lazy afternoons of playing hide-and-seek in the neighbors' azalea bushes and that breathless moment when "it" comes so close I can smell the summer sweat in my brother's hair, but he fails to find me in my green hideaway.

I am sure there was plenty of meanness, domestic violence, hunger, and abuse all around me. The magic of my family protected me. The sensibilities of my grandmother, a Swedish immigrant, and my father, a transplanted "Yankee," combined with my mother's love of this poor, rural county and entwined in my blood as deeply as the printer's ink of newspaper work.

George County was, and is, a very poor county. The societal ills that plague every community were all there, only hidden from me by family and a community that understood the importance of innocence—because it is such a rare and brief gift.

I enjoyed grammar school and my teachers. It wasn't uncommon for Mrs. Aaron or Mrs. Horne to invite schoolchildren to their homes as a special treat for a project well done or for good behavior. These patient teachers taught me and other students how to knit and make rag rugs. We learned these things after school hours.

As I remember, my teachers enjoyed our company, even after having us in the classroom for eight hours at a stretch. I suspect this had a lot to do with the fact that if I was disrespectful or ill-behaved in the schoolroom, I would pay a high price at home. My mother was all about mischief and pranks, but she had no tolerance for rudeness or cruelty.

Most of my old teachers are dead and gone now, as are the dirt roads where I galloped horses wild and free. Everything must be paved for fancy trucks that are a mockery of the vehicles once used on farms. Much of the old South that is forever blended with the word "Mississippi" is gone.

Still, I read the farm news, the want ads, the classifieds, the Internet land sales. I look in Stone and Perry counties, hoping for something next to the DeSoto National Forest. The rural stretches of the black prairie land around West Point call to me. Simpson County, near the Strong River, has much potential. The rolling terrain around Natchez and Vicksburg holds an element of enchantment. I'm not a big city gal, and thank goodness Mississippi doesn't offer a lot in that way. Each time I do a book signing in Starkville or Greenwood, Vicksburg or Natchez, I think about how wonderful it would be to live in an area with a thriving little town. I love the coastal counties, too, but not too close to the water. With horses, a storm like Katrina is simply too hard to endure for a second time.

One of my greatest joys is finding a piece of property for sale and going to explore it. Even though Mississippi is developing, there's still plenty of beautiful land. Maybe one day I'll find the property that serves as a portal back to the world of Mississippi that I yearn for. I'm sure it's there; I just have to find it. And whatever it costs, it'll be worth the price.

David Sheffield

David Sheffield began his screenwriting career as a writer for *Saturday Night Live*, where he contributed many of Eddie Murphy's most memorable sketches, including "Buckwheat," "Gumby," "Mr. Robinson's Neighborhood," and "James Brown's Celebrity Hot Tub Party." His movie credits—all shared with long-time writing partner Barry Blaustein—include *Coming to America*, *Boomerang*, and *The Nutty Professor*.

It was Africa hot in Jones County, Mississippi, the day the moving van rolled in from Los Angeles. Heat shimmered above the blacktop road, coaxing up little tar bubbles that crackled and popped under the wheels of the truck.

The driver, who had packed up our house in the Hollywood Hills, climbed down from the cab, took a look around at the weedy yard and rusting tin roof of our temporary digs and said, "Man, you made a move."

We had come home to rural Mississippi after twenty-five years in big-city Los Angeles to build ourselves a modest horse farm. All we wanted was a little peace and quiet. What we got instead was the Mayhews.

Cynthia and I paid them a call the day we drove out to scout our land. We parked the car in the scattershot shade of a big water oak in the Mayhews' front yard and warily approached the house, a homebuilt shotgun affair. A pack of rapacious curs sprang out from under the porch, barking their fool heads off.

Soon the Mayhews appeared, gunning their four-wheelers out of a canebrake, their twin machines spitting and growling as they came, automatic rifles strapped across the handlebars. Herbert Mayhew led the way, his corpulent mass tottering unsteadily on the four-wheeler. His wife, Bootsy, followed close behind, powering up the gravel drive, cotton housedress flapping in the breeze, a John Deere cap covering most of her brittle grey hair.

We explained who we were and that we had bought the adjoining two hundred acres from Cynthia's cousins with plans to clear twenty acres or so for our horse farm. The Mayhews were polite but chary, telling us all kinds of blood-curdling tales designed to scare us off our land.

"They's coyotes in there big as German shepherds," said Bootsy. "Them thangs will kill you." Her old eyes glittered at the thought of Cynthia and me being ripped to shreds.

"And rattlers? Hoo! You never seen the like of buzz-tails. Deadly, just deadly." Bootsy wrapped her bony arms around her shoulders and shivered for emphasis. All we needed was a cauldron and a couple of witchy sisters and we could have staged a backwoods production of *Macbeth*. Bootsy had the toil and trouble thing down.

Speaking of trouble, their grandson Jason had a patch of clover planted in the yard behind his ramshackle trailer. When deer wandered up to graze, the young sportsman aimed a high-powered rifle out of his kitchen window and cut loose. It was enough to make Ted Nugent shake his head in disgust.

It soon became clear that the Mayhews were using our land as a private hunting preserve, what Herbert called "keeping an eye on the place." We told them we were going in there to scout around.

"If y'all git lost, shoot three times and we'll come runnin'," said Herbert. I confessed we didn't have a gun. Herbert and Bootsy couldn't imagine such a thing. They regarded us with gentle pity, as though we were sure to be found later, faces gnawed beyond recognition.

We set out, wielding a couple of dull Chinese-made machetes from an army surplus store. One thing the Mayhews had not exaggerated was the forbidding nature of the terrain. We groped along dwindling game trails through piney woods so choked with brush, so booby-trapped with thorny vines we could barely make headway.

Finally, we blundered onto an old logging road that led us into the deeper woods along turgid Tiger Creek where bald cypress, turkey pines, red gum, and cottonwoods grew tall and the clay ground gave way to soggy mulch.

There stood the sagging remains of a camouflage shooting stand which overlooked a pile of shucked corn, and up in a tree, a large aluminum pan light powered by a couple of truck batteries. A perfect set-up for illegally potshotting deer at night. Clearly this kind of behavior was going to have to stop. Still, I was loath to confront the Mayhews.

Herbert and Bootsy romanced us with neighborly gestures: runty pears from the yard, greens from the garden, and a stack of firewood. We were invited to sit and talk on their screen porch under the hot blast of the rotating fan. Bootsy proudly pointed to the horns of several spike bucks she had shot with a .22 rifle kept propped by the kitchen door.

Herbert gave us a report on his trapping. "Finally caught that ol' bobcat that's been eatin' my ducks."

Bootsy was wide-eyed with concern. "How big was he?"

"About six foot long."

Bootsy sucked in her breath. "Now, that's big enough to *hurt* you."

Then Herbert got right to it. "Do you reckon it'd be all right if Jason and some of his friends was to hunt your land?"

I muttered something noncommittal but vaguely negative. "We were hoping to ride the horses over there without worrying about somebody shooting at us," I said, "but let me think about it."

Since she was local and bound to know, I asked our cowgirl helper, Kasey, her opinion of Jason Mayhew's friends.

"Jason and some of them boys decided they was going to round up a bunch of deer by drivin' em in a circle. Then they all started shootin' at once. It's like, what part of them being in a circle did they not git?"

The Mayhews had us pegged as hopelessly naïve city slickers who couldn't possibly know anything about guns or hunting, but they couldn't have been more wrong. In fact, the Sheffields have always been pretty handy with guns.

My great-grandfather, William Sylvester Sheffield, joined the Confederate Army at the age of thirteen and later served for many years as the pistol-packing sheriff of Itawamba County.

During the Great Depression, my father, Hubert Sheffield, hunted rabbits with rocks when he couldn't afford shotgun shells. For pocket money, he won bets by shooting quarters out of the air with a rifle. He paid his tuition at Mississippi College with a truckload of turnips for the school cafeteria. So if we Sheffields didn't exactly fall off a turnip truck, we damn near did.

Since my parents had to support seven kids on Mississippi schoolteacher salaries, we hunted and fished, not so much for sport as for survival.

All five of us boys were issued shotguns at an early age and sent out to shoot something edible. Our table fare included squirrel, rabbit, goose, duck, quail, dove, venison, and, on occasion, frog legs that twitched in the grease as Mother fried them.

The three older sons—known in the family as the "big boys"—had the first choice of weapons, leaving my younger brother, Buddy, and me the hand-me-downs. When I turned eleven I was bequeathed a single-barrel 16-gauge Stevens shotgun with black electrical tape wrapped around the stock.

As a teenager, my brother Emory invented a game called "Find the Hole." He would send us little ones into the hall where we'd wait on tenterhooks to hear the splat of his .22 rifle. Then we'd rush back into Emory's room hoping to be the first to find the fresh bullet hole in the ceiling.

Such was my Snopesy heritage. Who then was I to tell the Mayhews they couldn't hunt? I was wracked with guilt even thinking about it. Events would change my mind.

While we were out of town for the weekend, we left the place in the care of our son Morrison's girlfriend, a handsome young woman from Florida. She saddled my old horse, Zeus, and as she rode down the road past the trailer, Jason fired a shotgun. Zeus bolted, almost tossing her off.

Jason claimed he was aiming at a squirrel but nobody really believed him, not even Bootsy.

Then my worst fears were realized when Polar, our white Siberian husky and my favorite dog in the whole world, crawled under our fence, wandered over to the Mayhews' woods and got caught in one of Herbert's coyote traps. Polar spent a desperate couple of hours trying to free himself by gnawing on the trap. He wore down his canines but was otherwise unharmed.

That did it. I posted our property, nailing up bright yellow "No Hunting" signs out on the highway, down by the creek, and along the half-mile border between the Mayhews and us.

There followed a deep chill in relations with the Mayhews.

Banished from hunting, young Jason fired round after round at a target in the yard, his big-bore rifle thundering like a howitzer. Shots rattled our windows and stirred the horses to near panic. Our dogs trembled and hid under the bed. Jason claimed to be "sighting in" his scope but obviously he was shooting to intimidate us, hoping the city folks would give up and slink back to Los Angeles. This was getting out of hand.

My good friend Reed drove up from Biloxi, the trunk of his BMW loaded with firearms.

"You've got to return fire," he explained. "Let the Mayhews know they're not the only ones with guns."

Reed and I headed out to the woods where we blasted away with everything we had, including a sawed-off pump shotgun, a .44 magnum revolver, a .9-millimeter Glock, and an M-4 assault rifle. It sounded like Pickett's charge. The ground was littered with spent shells. I started to pick them up.

"No," said Reed. "Leave the empties so they'll know what we've got."

Work on the farm progressed apace. We cleared pastures, dug a three-acre pond, built a cabin for us and a fine cypress barn for the horses.

For a while we observed a fragile cease-fire with the Mayhews. Then we began to notice a new presence at Jason's trailer. A pretty, if somewhat plump, local girl took up with him. Jason started to disappear for days at a time. The rumor was he had found a job cleaning up after the BP oil spill in the gulf.

There were peaceful overtures from the Mayhews. Bootsy sent over a dozen small brown eggs and a jar of peach preserves. We responded with a ham at Christmas. As time wore on, we resumed waving politely to each other as we passed on the road.

Then came the blessed day when I spotted Jason walking slow circles in his yard, cradling on his shoulder a newborn baby Mayhew, already suited up in a little camo onesie. All shooting ceased. Peace had been restored by the charms of domesticity, and once again, Woman had fulfilled her essential role as enforcer of the peace, a boon to mankind unchanged since the days of Aristophanes.

Today harmony reigns over our farm, a peaceable kingdom. Horses graze lazily in the sun, oftentimes sharing the pasture with a flock of wild turkeys. Squirrels scamper and doves fly free. Possums, coons, and rabbits forage without fear. Deer wander unmolested.

My friend Reed shows up with a turkey call and a shotgun, asking if he can hunt. I tell him he'll have to shoot me first.

Ronnie Riggs

Ronnie Riggs was born in Laurel and grew up in Baton Rouge, Louisiana, and Hattiesburg. He graduated from the University of Mississippi, lived and worked in New Orleans for a few years, then moved to Mobile, Alabama, where he earned an MBA and became a CPA. He has held various managerial positions in industry accounting. He and his wife are the parents of two sons. He returns to Mississippi regularly to remember, visit, and decorate the graves of his ancestors, and he is the proud owner of six shady burial plots in the city of Hattiesburg where he plans to get some rest one day.

Early morning Mississippi sun sparkled down through branches covering the road ahead and I drove slowly, struggling to find a cemetery where there appeared to be none. I'd driven a thousand miles from my home in Maryland down to Mississippi, my birthplace, hoping to uncover a significant new layer of my family history. It seems no matter how far we roam from home there will always be ties pulling us back there, and so it has always been for me. I was here looking for the graves of long-gone distant relatives I had never known.

I'd driven the road once, and, having found nothing, had turned back to give it another go. I checked the road name and knew I was definitely in the right place, but it sure didn't seem there was any cemetery here. The road was mostly woods and was only a mile and a half long start to finish, then it dead-ended into another small country road. So there wasn't much area to search. The man who had told me where to find the graves had given me a name, "the Old Enon Cemetery," he'd said, so I guessed I wasn't looking for something that was completely overgrown back in the woods. Still, I wasn't finding it. Here a small ranch house with a menacing dog circling inside a chain-link fence, there a cleared area where three or four logging trucks were parked— but nowhere a cemetery.

I crossed a set of railroad tracks and considered a small white block building I hadn't noted before. It looked like it might be one of the VFW buildings so typical in rural Mississippi, but as I gave it a closer look I realized it was a small church. It seemed a church ought to have a cemetery, so I parked, walked around back, and there it was—the Old Enon Cemetery. A search that I'd begun months earlier from my home in Maryland had led me here to this small cemetery behind the Endtime Jesus Name Church in rural Mississippi, the place where I hoped to uncover another layer of my own Mississippi family history.

There wasn't a lot of oral family history passed down to me, but there was some. I was raised by my grandparents and so I heard and learned more than I might have otherwise, simply by virtue of my as-sociation with an older generation. Even so, I knew the history of my family surname, Riggs, only back to my grandfather's father, Porter M. Riggs, who had lived and died in Perry County, Mississippi. Porter Riggs had been born in 1864 and died in 1954, three years before I was born. I knew little else about him besides the fact that he had been a farmer, was married to Nancy Narcissus Riggs, and had home-steaded what we grew up calling "the old place," 120 acres of land in Perry County. Porter and Nancy Riggs and most of their six children are buried at the Seminary Baptist Church in Perry County, just a few miles from "the old place," and I grew up visiting their graves with my grandfather. From my family's oral history I understood Porter Riggs had moved south from somewhere "up north," and since no one had ever seemed to know where "up north," I'd assumed the trail ran cold before him.

With age I've become much more interested in my history, and with the Internet, information that once would have been almost impos-sible to uncover is often now just a few clicks away. I'd started searching online some months before this June Mississippi morning, and had been amazed to discover Porter Riggs didn't come from "up north" at all; he'd been born right in the heart of Mississippi. Old census records from the 1800s showed Porter Riggs had been born and raised "on Black Creek" and had grown up there as one of ten children born to Joseph R. Riggs and Cecilia Ann Weldy Riggs. After diligently searching old cemetery records for Perry County and e-mailing anyone I thought could help me, I had learned that Joseph and Cecilia Riggs were buried here, at the Old Enon Cemetery. It was as if once I began blowing the accumulated years of dust from the history books, they fell open, exactly to my chapter, and so much was revealed. I learned Joseph Riggs (b. 12/16/1812, d. 3/08/1899) had been a schoolteacher, an unusual occupation for a man of farming age in the rural agrarian economy of 1800s Mississippi. From this I surmised he was probably better educated than was typical for his time. I learned he was twenty-three years older than his wife, and that they had married on June 23, 1855, in Harrison County, Mississippi, when he was forty-two and she was nineteen. Perhaps most fascinating, I learned that Joseph Riggs had gone off to fight for the Mississippi Cavalry during the Civil War when he was in his early fifties. How amazing to see the years peel away and begin to learn long-lost details of family history!

All my research and efforts had brought me now to the Old Enon Cemetery, where I found the graves of Joseph and Cecilia Riggs, my great-great-grandparents. They are buried in the very back of that cemetery, their graves abutting woods. When I found the graves they were almost completely overtaken by the undergrowth and extending tree branches, and it took me several visits and much work to clear them. Once they were cleared I brought flowers—a thing I'm sure their graves hadn't had for many years—and took a few pictures. Buried alongside Joseph and Cecilia is a daughter, Elizabeth Riggs Cluff, who died at the age of thirty-three. I stood contemplating what had taken Elizabeth's life so early and how sad it must have been for her parents to bury her so young. And why hadn't she been buried elsewhere, alongside Mr. Cluff? So many unanswered questions, and yet so many that are now answered. I've learned that it was actually Joseph Riggs, my great-great-grandfather, who was the first of my ancestors in Mississippi. He is the one my great-aunt spoke of who came from "up north," only "up north" had turned out to be "due east," a small South Carolina town called Walterboro. I now know that back in Walterboro—in 1834—Joseph's father, Thomas Riggs, was one of the founders of Walterborough Academy, the forerunner of Walterboro's current city school system. This helped me make sense of why Joseph Riggs had been listed in the 1870 Mississippi census records as a "schoolteacher." He came to that profession honestly, having had a father for whom education was clearly very important. I also learned that, in addition to being a founding father of the Walterborough Academy, Thomas Riggs was something akin to the tax collector in 1800s Walterboro. Through my research I'd found numerous 1800s Walterboro tax returns that were signed and attested to by Thomas Riggs. As I am a CPA myself, imagine what a connection I feel with that piece of information! I'd often thought what an interesting given name my great-grandfather, Porter, had. Other than Porter Wagoner, I've never seen the name used as a first name. That became clear too when I learned that Cecilia Weldy Riggs, Porter's mother, had a younger brother named Porter after whom she obviously had named her own son, my great-grandfather. It was like a puzzle you'd worked on for years with little progress; then suddenly you get up one day and find exactly the right spot for a dozen pieces.

It takes most of us many years, I think, to reach a maturity level where these things matter to us, where they become important. As a youngster I made many Mississippi cemetery visits with my grandparents, especially around the holidays each year. I didn't much question what we were doing, but I certainly wasn't very interested. We'd go, taking fire ant poison and plastic flowers from Fred's Dollar Store. Old flowers would be cleared away. If they looked like they still had some life in them my grandmother would take them home, spray-paint them, and hold them for the next cemetery trip. Fire ant poison would be sprinkled liberally as needed, weeds were pulled, and new flowers were put out. Usually, stories were told about the person whose grave we were working on—some anecdote, some fond memory my grandparents had. Through these stories I came to feel I knew them all, even the ones who had died before I was born. When we went to my grand-mother's sister's grave in Hattiesburg my grandmother usually told the story of how her sister had run away at sixteen to marry the young man she loved. Their parents learned of the plan and went to bring her home. When they found their sixteen-year-old daughter she told them she loved him, and if they made her come back home she'd only run away again, and she'd keep running away until she married him. Faced with such unyielding determination her parents relented and the young lovers married. They raised three children of their own and remained together until parted by death many years later. I may be the only person alive today who can stand at Virgie McCrory's grave and know this about her. It's a useless scrap of information that crumbled to dust many, many years ago, but I never put flowers on her grave without hearing my grandmother tell that story in my head.

At Seminary Baptist Church is the grave of Alla Riggs Hinton, a great-aunt who died many years before I was born. Buried next to Alla is her "infant son" who was born—and died—on August 12, 1920. Alla herself died three days later on August 15, 1920. My grandfather, who was Alla's brother, always said she'd given birth at home and something went wrong. They couldn't get a doctor to her, he'd say, and—by the time they did—it was too late for both Alla and the child. Such stories these are, lives lived in a sometimes harsh, unforgiving world. It's fas-cinating to consider that every grave represents a complete life lived, a complete story lost in time.

My grandparents are long since gone now as well, and on my annual trips back to Mississippi theirs are the graves I visit and take flowers to first. There are a number of others I visit as well, all those we went to when I was a child. In some cases I knew the people whose graves I visited; in some cases I never did. But having now regularly visited their graves over the fifty-four years of my own life they have become important to me and I cannot walk away from the responsibility and kinship I feel for them. I've now added the graves of Joseph Riggs, Ce-cilia Riggs, and Elizabeth Riggs Cluff to my list. I think to take such a responsibility on in a meaningful way requires one to be closer to death than to birth. The pendulum has to have swung far enough that you can see yourself there one day. I've reached that point, and so I'm honored to do for these distant relatives what they cannot and what no one else will; I try to give them some dignity in death. It's an attempt to reach across the years and say, "You are not forgotten."

Years ago on our honeymoon, my wife and I walked one cold, grey winter afternoon through an old cemetery in Cade's Cove, Tennessee, and the epitaph on one particular grave caught my attention and has remained in my memory since:

> Remember friends, as you pass by
> As you are now, so once was I.
> As I am now, you're sure to be
> Prepare yourself to follow me.

These lines summarize well what I've come to believe about family history, searching for roots and honoring the dead. We must honor them, and we must prepare ourselves to follow them. Someday I'll be buried in one of those Mississippi cemeteries, and I hope, occasionally, someone will stop by—to place some flowers—to remember me.

Charline R. McCord

Charline R. McCord was born in Hattiesburg and grew up in Laurel and Jackson, Tennessee. She holds a Ph.D. in English from the University of Southern Mississippi and bachelor's and master's degrees from Mississippi College, where she won the Bellamann Award for Creative Writing, edited the literary magazine, and was named 2009 Distinguished Alumna by the Mississippi College Department of English. She has coedited a series of eight books, four of them featuring outstanding Mississippians, with Judy H. Tucker.

I was tricked into leaving Mississippi, and it was a very clever trick that no twelve-year-old would've ever seen coming. I owned a town at the time and the trick took that town away from me, or me from it. I had never had the first thought of leaving home, unlike my older brother, the trickster, who once ran away from home with a friend and spent a whole night sleeping in a concrete culvert by the railroad track. Why is it that every boy who reads *The Adventures of Huckleberry Finn* thinks he has to "light out for the territory" to demonstrate his bravery and independence? I knew Huck Finn was to blame; after all, the unbaptized raft my brother built was floating in a sea of grass in our backyard. I was still too young to comprehend that a father with Pap Finn leanings probably provided a better explanation of the current state of affairs.

The trickster's disappearance was a high drama time with enormous potential. My mother had to do something she never did; she left her job and came home in a furor. She snatched up the phone and made a string of calls, paced the floor smoking Marlboros, and swore she would kill him on sight the minute he came through the door. I believed her; my mother was a rock before the arrival of steel magnolias, so I took a seat in the living room and waited quietly, fearful my older brother might be enough of a trickster to somehow know not to return and accept the killing. I wondered if he was hiding in the alley behind our house, swaying on a high limb in the top of the mulberry tree, or lying beneath a sheet like a dead man inside his clubhouse built like a casket. I had found him in all these places and figured I could find him now if I wanted to, but I didn't want to. I wanted this crime to play out in a natural way, one that resulted in well-deserved punishment.

I wondered whether he would shimmy his guilt-ridden body through a darkened bedroom window or brazenly stride in the front door like absolutely nothing had happened. I abandoned my post just long enough to be sure all the windows were locked, and then I returned to my seat to wait. I would not help to find him; I would not be lured into his latest plot. I was the good child; I would simply witness his killing, testify truthfully that it was a justifiable homicide, and go on with my life. I scanned the room and kept watch on all possible entries, my mood heightened by the passage of time and my mother's voice continuing on the phone in the background. She voiced an odd mixture of anger and concern late into the night, providing a comforting signal that the drama was very much alive and well. I fell asleep on the sofa in my clothes and she never seemed to notice.

It was the afternoon of the second day when he returned; walked right through the front door acting like he still had a right to claim *this* house and *this* family—just as I expected he would. I watched my mother, the would-be murderer, race toward the front door, catch sight of her firstborn, prodigal son, and immediately drop to her knees on the glossy linoleum floor and sob, all the starch flowing right out of her. At that moment I knew I had a new mother, a weaker mother, a mother that would never again rise up with the force of a tornado and utter death threats that she truly meant to fulfill. It was a monumental day of sadness in my life that I still remember vividly. The trickster had won. There was no killing. We had him back and from all appearances he had tripled his value where Mother was concerned. That all happened on 8th Avenue in Laurel, the town I completely owned, before the next trick that banished me.

The year was 1961, and I was busy wrapping up the seventh grade at Jones Junior High School. I had only a vague awareness of the troubles that were brewing elsewhere in the South; I had heard classmates bantering about the line "Don't mess with Mississippi." One evening my mother called me in the kitchen and informed me I was going on a summer vacation. I was immediately suspicious; my family didn't take vacations. I bombarded her with questions. Eventually, I learned I was going to Jackson, Tennessee, to visit my great-aunt and great-uncle. Never mind that I didn't know this great-aunt and great-uncle and had never once asked to go visit them. I was told they were eager to see me, and the most amazing part was the news that I was traveling alone—my own personal vacation. I explained that I didn't want a personal vacation; I wanted to spend the summer with friends at the Daphne Park swimming pool, as I did every year. I couldn't believe I had to explain to my mother that seventh-grade girls don't vacation alone! She said it was all worked out and I would not be vacationing *alone*; I would be visiting my great-aunt and great-uncle. She assured me it was perfectly respectable for family members to visit one another in this fashion, and that I would be traveling on a Greyhound bus! I resisted, but she did not fold to the floor in my behalf, and in the end there was nothing to do but accept my surprise personal vacation as if it was a shiny game show giveaway.

As my departure date grew nearer, my mother's concerns increased and she began to give me a number of instructions about what I was and was not to do during my bus ride to Jackson. I must sit up front on the seat immediately behind the bus driver. I must not talk to strangers. I should not get off the bus when it stopped unless I absolutely had to. I must keep my bag in the seat right beside me and watch it at all times. On and on she went, issuing more frantic instructions with each passing day until finally, on the day I was to leave, the truth tumbled out. She had bought the bus ticket for the trickster, my older brother.

He was the one who was supposed to ride the Greyhound to Tennessee. She had devised a reward program, offered it to him in good faith, and purchased it in advance to prove the trip was his if only he would study, pull up his grades, and cross the ninth-grade finish line. Just across that line sat *his* own personal summer vacation, a chance to light out for the territory via Greyhound bus all the way from Laurel, Mississippi, to Jackson, Tennessee. But just as I did, the trickster had his own ideas about how he wanted to spend his summer, and his response was to ensure that he was hand-picked to finish the ninth grade in summer school. There could be no solo vacation for him; he wasn't available to travel. He skulked around grinning as my suitcase was packed and I was readied for departure. It was like a blastoff—an exciting new way to unload a pesky, younger sister. What I didn't know until later, and what the trickster couldn't have known either, was that I had a one-way ticket. I lost a family, a town, and a state on my 1961 "summer vacation." I was twelve years old, and it would be sixteen years before I got a return trip to reclaim my home state.

In Tennessee my status was elevated to that of an only child. My great-aunt and great-uncle had no children of their own, a thing that was fairly obvious as I gradually discovered all that they did not know about a young person. Nonetheless, I was reasonably entertained. My aunt was a world-class shopper; she had converted a room into a walk-in closet and had a wardrobe that would rival those of the stars. She took me into department stores and explained why the fabric in this dress or sweater was high quality and the fabric in another one was simply not. Her aunt Beulah owned a millinery shop in downtown Jackson and it was a special treat when we stopped by there. While my aunt visited with her aunt, I occupied myself by trying on every style and color of hat in the store.

Soon my aunt and uncle sought permission to extend my two-week vacation, and the two weeks were stretched to cover the entire summer, and then my eighth-grade school year. I missed my family deeply, and this is the time I can point to when my writing began in earnest. At the age of twelve I embraced the act of writing, sometimes penning as many as twelve or fifteen letters a week. I worked hard to maintain a lifeline with my family—to capture my reader's attention, to tell them an interesting story, to entertain them, to regularly put a part of me on paper and mail it home to Mississippi, not only to remind them of my continued northern existence, but, more importantly, to force my way into the daily lives of those I loved and elicit some response that confirmed they had not forgotten me.

I became aware that my aunt and uncle were asking me frequent and specific questions about my life in Laurel, my absent father, my hard-working mother, my older and younger brothers, what kind of support we had in our lives from neighbors and our church family. This information was gathered and rehashed in other closed discussions that I was not a part of. At one point my uncle and his brother made a road trip to Laurel to check on my family; I found out about it upon their return and wondered why they didn't take me along. Eventually, I learned that my mother wasn't well, and that steps were being taken to arrange for her care as well as that of my two brothers. I was going to stay in Tennessee where I was, my younger brother would be going to Louisiana to live with grandparents, and my older brother would go for a time to another aunt and uncle in Arkansas. The prevailing feeling was that the situation was definitely temporary, and eventually our fragmented family would be reassembled. I continued to write letters to keep that dream alive.

In 1966, I graduated from high school and went to work for WBBJ Television in Jackson, Tennessee. Like all high school graduates, I was eager to move out and experience the world on my own. By this point I had been independent of my immediate family in many ways for five years. I met a friend at church who was looking for a roommate; she was fresh out of a brief marriage and had a car and a house full of furniture. I had neither; my contribution was the one thing she lacked—a top-notch stereo system and lots of albums. I helped her get a job at the television station, and we had a fine time enjoying youth and freedom until a high school friend sent me a letter imploring me to agree to a date with her brother-in-law, Bob McCord. There was only one small hitch (isn't there always?). He was twelve years my senior, she reported,

but "a really likeable guy!" I thought she had surely lost her mind; I had
no desire to date one so ancient, but I relented, fully intending to go
out once and once only, then check "favor to friend" off my list. Several
months later we were still dating, and Bob McCord showed up one
evening, sat on our living room sofa wearing a grave demeanor and began a halting enumeration of his debts—he owed a couple of hundred
to a men's clothing store, he owed the bank for his car, he thought he
might owe his mother a little. I was reasonably adept at reading people
and I could see precisely where this was going. This older man was
on the verge of asking me for a loan! I could listen patiently and try
to sympathize, but the answer was predetermined. I had no money
and little choice but to conclude that he was not only too old and too
broke but also too ignorant if he didn't already know that. Suddenly
he delivered his question: "Now, knowing all this, will you marry me?"
Gears ground to a halt, switched, and what came out of my mouth
was a question that dove to the heart of the matter: "How long do you
think it will take you to pay all that off?" I owned little—my clothes
and a good stereo system—but I had no debt and I wasn't looking to
share anybody else's.

We were married on December 27, 1968, and happily settled in
the small town of Humboldt, Tennessee, home to the West Tennessee Strawberry Festival and the writer Jesse Hill Ford, known for his
1965 novel-turned-movie, *The Liberation of Lord Byron Jones*. On the
night of November 16, 1970, Ford turned Humboldt and the law firm I
worked for upside down by shooting into a car parked on his property,
resulting in the death of army private George H. Doaks, a young black
man. In July 1971, Ford's highly publicized trial came to a close with
his acquittal, and scores of curious spectators rose from the sofas and
chairs of our law office, where they had overflowed and camped daily
seeking refuge from a packed and sweltering courtroom, and began
their journey out of town. The verdict was unsatisfactory to many, and
the experience would haunt Jesse Hill Ford until his death by suicide
on June 1, 1996.

One month after the trial, our first daughter, Tracy, was born, followed by Lisa in 1974. That same year I enrolled in classes at nearby

Jackson State Community College, and life was calm until 1976, when, very abruptly, Wayne Knitting Mill, my husband's employer for fourteen years, closed its Humboldt doors. Bob was a native west Tennessean who was intimate with game and fish, woods and lakes, and he had no desire to leave the place where he'd spent a lifetime hunting and fishing alongside family and friends. Nonetheless, when a former co-worker and fishing buddy called and encouraged him to send his resume to Hanes Hosiery, he did so, and before long he was offered a sales territory in the heart of the Magnolia State—Jackson, Mississippi!

The day I heard this exciting news I spread a Mississippi map out on the dining room table and hovered over it until I had selected the town of Clinton—a college town, since I was still working on a bachelor's degree—to be my new home. In January of 1977, we watched as our belongings were loaded into a Mayflower truck, ran the vacuum through the house one last time as a courtesy to the new owners, and left Humboldt for Clinton. Mississippi got snow that January and somewhere north of Jackson we caught up with our Mayflower truck; it was broken down on the side of Interstate 55 and wouldn't show up in Clinton until late the next day.

But what's one more day when you're already sixteen years late coming home? In the wisdom and words of Shakespeare, "All's well that ends well." I've been back in Mississippi for thirty-five years now—the official score is Mississippi 47, Tennessee 16. And as far as I can tell I'm here to stay—older, wiser, and hopefully too smart to be tricked out of here again. Regrets? Both my children were born in Tennessee. Rewards? All four grandchildren were born in Mississippi. Lessons learned? A two-week vacation in Tennessee bears a curious resemblance to Mississippi kudzu. Final thoughts? I feel a special kinship with the biblical Job—everything that was taken away has been given back—twice as much as I had before. Thanks be to God!

Barry Hannah

Barry Hannah was born in Meridian and grew up in Clinton. He earned a bachelor of arts from Mississippi College and a master of arts and master of fine arts in creative writing from the University of Arkansas. Hannah taught creative writing at numerous colleges and universities and was writer-in-residence at the University of Mississippi at the time of his death on March 1, 2010. He was the recipient of the Bellamann Award for Creative Writing, the Arnold Gingrich Award in short fiction, a special award for literature from the American Institute of Arts and Letters, and a Guggenheim Fellowship. He also served as judge for the Nelson Algren Award and the American Book Award. Hannah's works have been nominated for both the National Book Award (*Geronimo Rex*, 1972) and the Pulitzer Prize (*High Lonesome*, 1996).

I see them pass still, the little old tiny-headed women of Clinton, Mississippi, in the '50s, in their giant cars on the brick streets. Or on their porches or at their azalea beds scolding dogs, then me; nestled in the pews and bobbing heads in the aisles of the church. Bringing in their covered dishes to church suppers. They established the tone of my world. All of them ancient beyond years now or dead. They observed and accounted. I fled them; I was a creature of the night, a little sinner. Or was I only paranoid, like the biblical thief who fleeth when none pursueth? Those days when they were big, these women, in my youth. But now I see their replicates in my grown town, don't I? I always wanted to explain to them how they didn't know how it was, they hadn't the faintest. I picked up the rhythms of Scripture for my tales,

I'm certain, but it was mystery and sin that had me. I was not the echo for the voices of the tiny-headed women. Was not antiphonal to their voices. I was the dreadful opposite voice to whatever they asserted, the polar howling wretch. In Baptist songs I always liked where you were a wretch or a worm or, just as I am, hopeless.

But many of the women were kind, too kind, to me. Mrs. Bunyard in the third grade, she encouraged my tales and lies, as long as I wrote them down. Even at the same time she made you wash out your mouth with hard soap for swearing, or even for finding humor in the term *jackass*. This was in the good days when teachers listened patiently to your explanations, then beat hell out of you with a holed board. Fiction is work, and I suppose there would be no fiction in the Garden of Eden until the apple and the fall. Begins the mystery of evil, or of the Other. And the making of books of which there is no end, as warned in Ecclesiastes.

Like many Mississippians, I shied away from Faulkner, who was at once remote and right there in your own backyard, the powerful resident alien. Having read a little of him, I sensed I would be overcome by him, and had a dread, in fact, that he might be the last word. That I would wind up a pining third-rate echo, like many another Southerner.

I finally had a real story at age twenty-three up at Fayetteville, Arkansas.

This followed a near religious conversion tedious to everybody but me, I'd guess. I'll only say that I became more committed to people who could never tell their own stories and that I was no longer ashamed of being from the most derided state in the Union.

Another time I was fishing one Saturday afternoon with my father, nephews, and my small oldest son Po, who was afire with Jimi Hendrix at the time. We were catching big bass, all of us up and down the dam, with minnows on cane poles. My father sat there in his lawn chair with his vodka and his cigar, king of the hill. All the nephews, his grandchildren, rushing to bait his hook as he presided there. I had a novel out after enormous work. It had been celebrated widely, although it sold nothing, and I was a whole man. The sun went behind a cloud and the wind went up, and we were almost dark, in a sudden chilly breeze, a momentary violent change almost as if to another, northern geography. In July, out of the heat, it seemed pure magic, and it felt wonderful. I knelt there consumed by a decision. A huge bass suddenly grabbed my line. I went into a spiritual ecstasy. My family was all around me, we were in heaven. You could cut the joy with a knife. We all felt it, although nobody spoke. This is it, this is it, my life! To say good stuff, like this. To say it, maybe so well they won't forget. This is it. Thanks to God. Later, before his death, my father told me he had never had a better day. He had caught a seven-pound bass, the family record. But that's not what I mean, son, he said. The other day my son, out of nowhere, asked me, Dad, you remember that day on Elwood Ratliff's dam?

Jesmyn Ward

Jesmyn Ward is a former Stegner Fellow at Stanford University and a Grisham Writer-in-Residence at the University of Mississippi. Her novels, *Where the Line Bleeds* and *Salvage the Bones*, are both set on the Mississippi coast where she grew up. *Salvage the Bones* is the 2011 winner of the National Book Award in fiction. Bloomsbury will publish her memoir about an epidemic of deaths of young black men in her community. She is an assistant professor at the University of South Alabama.

When my parents were young adults, they decided to return to Mississippi, where they were both from, with their two young children: my brother and me. They decided that a life in Mississippi was what they wanted, and they wanted to raise their children in the South. I was actually born in Berkeley, California, and when we moved home, I was three. As I grew older, I wondered about their decision, wondered what our lives would have been like if our parents had decided to raise us in California.

My teenage years had been rough, and I'd suffered and agonized over who I was and where I lived in the same ways that I suppose all teenagers suffer and agonize. Of course, my time had been complicated by the fact that I was black, and also the fact that I came from a poor family, and also by the fact that I went to a high school where most of the students were not black or poor. A sense of promise seemed to exist only in the outside world, the world outside of the state, and I was eager to pursue it. So when I graduated from high school, I left

Mississippi for college in California. And after California, I went to New York for my first job, and after New York, I went to Michigan for graduate school, and after there, I went back to California for a writing fellowship.

From the moment I'd first seen the expanse of the Pacific Ocean stretching out over the horizon from a plane window at the age of twelve, I'd associated the West with possibility. There was something about the way the water stretched out into the distance, on and on, the way I imagined it wrapping around the world. *All those places*, I thought, *all those people.* I wanted to see them all, and when I returned to Mississippi at the end of the summer from visiting relatives in Oakland, I could not stop imagining those people and places. It was only when I was older that I realized that seeing the Pacific for the first time was an echo of another wonderment at the West, my first: standing at the edge of a road that ran east and west in front of my grandmother's house in Mississippi, barefoot, watching the sun set through the oaks, the sky burning red and pink and orange. I was eight, and I knew beauty.

My family wasn't happy about my leaving and choosing to attend college in California. They loved me, and they didn't want me to stray so far away from them. But I went because I felt I had to find opportunity. The world taught me that there are many people, and many places, that those things can afford pain or kindness. The world taught me that when I traveled outside of the United States for the first time to Oxford, England, I would meet a kind blonde stranger on the bus from London to Oxford, and that she would patiently tell me where I should transfer, how far away my stop would be, where I should get off, and how long it would take me to get to my final destination. The world also taught me that I would walk the streets of New York and encounter strangers who would give their seats to me on the subway after I fainted, but that there were also other strangers, men, who would brandish knives on the subway, who would shout insults at me when I refused to speak to them on the streets. I found a multitude of strangers in the world, some of them friends, some of them not.

As I traveled farther, I found success and beauty, but I found something else as well: a sense of emptiness undercut by sorrow. My family, whom I'd left in Mississippi, changed. My brother died when he was hit by a drunk driver. My sisters grew into women, bore children. My parents grew older. My grandmother's hair turned from salt and pepper gray to a stunning silver white, so beautiful that random people stop her in grocery stores, tell her: *you have beautiful hair.* And I missed them. I spent hours working, and during my empty moments, I could only think of them. So I began to think of returning home, and then I began searching for a way to make it happen. When I got a job at home, even though it was a temporary one, I took it.

On my last day in California, I stood on a cliff in San Francisco. I put my arms on the wooden railing and hunkered down in my jacket, seeking shelter under the evergreens which bent over me, twisted by the ocean wind and genetics, and I looked out at the water spreading westward and swallowing up the whole world. And I thought about the islands in the middle of the ocean, and the east there on the other side, and it was then I knew that I'd traveled far enough west to return to where I began, that I'd gone around the world far enough to return home.

When I returned home to Mississippi, I found that the possibility I'd imagined in the west existed in Mississippi, just as it existed in the wider world. I could be an adult, be a writer, an artist, have a family, and be surrounded by all that I loved in Mississippi. I found that through writing about what I'd hated about Mississippi as a teenager, I was able to live there as an adult.

Dolphus Weary

Dolphus Weary, president of R.E.A.L. Christian Foundation in Richland, holds degrees from Los Angeles Baptist College, Los Angeles Baptist Seminary, and the University of Southern Mississippi in addition to the doctor of ministry degree from Reformed Theological Seminary in Jackson, Mississippi. He has also received four honorary doctoral degrees and the Meritorious Leadership Award from Tougaloo College, and he was inducted into the Alumni Hall of Fame at the University of Southern Mississippi. Weary continues to serve on national and local boards of directors. He is the author of a memoir of his young life entitled *I Ain't Coming Back*.

Dolphus Weary, August 7, 1946. The midwife couldn't spell very well, and she never was sure of the date. But she did a fine job helping my mother bring me into the world.

I was born in a run-down house somewhere near the one-store hamlet of Sandy Hook, Mississippi, not far from the Louisiana border.

When I was two, our family moved back to my mother's birthplace near D'Lo about thirty miles south of Jackson. D'Lo was supposedly named in the 1920s by a railroad conductor who had always called it "that damn low spot in the road." The U.S. Post Office cleaned it up to "D'Lo."

My father got discouraged when his income from sharecropping in that area didn't improve, so he left my mother and eight children and went back to Louisiana. He never came back, except for one brief visit.

If you had come to visit us then, you'd have traveled down old U.S.

Highway 49, a two-lane road that ran from Jackson to the Gulf Coast. It linked our rural county to the larger world. After driving through D'Lo, you'd have turned down a dirt road and gone a few more miles to the Gum Springs community. About five hundred feet up on the side of the hill was an unpainted wood shotgun house: three rooms and a porch.

We had no running water or plumbing. That meant lots of trips to a spring about a half mile through the woods. A few yards from the shack was an outhouse.

Such was home for me, my mother, Lucille, and my seven brothers and sisters. Mama called us her "stair steps."

I have warm memories of my family, but it was a constant struggle for us just to survive. We had no steady source of income. Mama did whatever she could to earn money. She washed clothes for white people, she scrubbed their floors. She cleaned eggs at a poultry house up the road, and of course she farmed. Her father lived across the road, and our house was surrounded by his four acres of cotton and five acres of corn.

Picking cotton season began in late August and ended right before Thanksgiving. Once we got Grandpa's cotton picked, we went to work for white folks who came in trucks to take us to their fields. They paid us two and a half cents a pound. My brother Melvin boasted that he could pick four hundred pounds a day. But I doubted it. Three hundred pounds would be an incredible day.

Education meant everything to Mama. She believed in her children going to school, and she always worked to see that we stayed in school. She didn't want us going through life the way she had, struggling to get by. People got to where they'd say, "Oh, Lucille is education crazy." It wasn't until I was grown-up and saw the big picture of segregation that I understood what a courageous thing my mother was doing. Most of the white landowners had no interest in seeing a black person get an education. Education meant freedom for blacks. But it meant that the white man would lose his source of cheap labor. Further, it meant that he couldn't treat black folk as dumb niggers and cheat them out of money and such.

Mama's great-grandmother, Emily Dixon, had been a slave. She died in 1940. She was at least twenty-one at the time of Lincoln's Emancipation Proclamation, and like the rest of the freed slaves, she was given forty acres and a mule to homestead. Later she willed the land to her granddaughter—my mama's mother. Mama had a number of years to be around her, and she passed down many stories about slavery.

When the book *Roots* was made into the successful TV miniseries, it was a very important experience for us as blacks. It took that tragic experience and somehow transformed it into a deep, positive experience of pride. The feeling was that as a people, we survived a terrible thing, similar to the way many Jews survived Nazi Germany.

But as a teenager thinking about what I was going to do with my life, I didn't feel any pride in being black. I'm surprised I didn't just end up angry. Certainly all the reasons were there why I should have. I'd heard the stories about Mama's great-grandma as a slave. I'd heard about the lynching of my grandma's boyfriend by the men in Braxton. I'd seen my own mother locked up in jail for no reason. I'd been cheated myself by white farmers.

I knew the system was hopelessly stacked against me. No matter what I might do, nothing was going to change. The only way out, it seemed to me, was the one so many blacks took—to go somewhere else and start all over. Just forget Mississippi. All I wanted to do was to get out and live my life. I didn't know how I'd get out. But I swore, "Someday I will. And when I do—I ain't never comin' back."

It was one thing to decide I was going to leave Mississippi. Figuring out *how* was something else. I had no developed skills, no money, not even a high school diploma yet. Still, my mind was made up. So every day I played different schemes over and over in my head, thinking about how to get out.

My role model was John Perkins. His ministry in Mendenhall was moving forward. During the mornings he farmed, and in the afternoons and evenings he led Bible studies and other activities at schools in four counties. He also visited people's homes to read the Bible, pray, and help in whatever way he could. I developed a vague idea that I wanted to do something similar to John and the others at the ministry.

To me, that meant finishing my education at a Christian college. There was just one problem—I didn't know a single accredited four-year Christian college that would admit a black person. I knew some Bible institutes that educated blacks. But I wanted a full college education as well as Bible instruction.

In the end, I decided that the only way out was to somehow get an education, and if I didn't get back in school right away, I never would. So I went to the Piney Woods School to see if they might have an opening. They told me they had a place, and I hurried over to the coach to claim a basketball scholarship.

Being in an academic setting, I became more aware of social and political issues and the people behind them. I learned more about the burgeoning civil rights movement and the hope that it offered black people. When Medgar Evers was gunned down on the doorstep of his home, it made me stop and think about my own life and how dangerous it had become to be a black in Mississippi. In response, I renewed my determination to get out of the state as soon as I finished at Piney Woods.

In my second year of junior college at Piney Woods, that opportunity presented itself when a group of young men from California spoke in chapel. When they invited students to talk with them after chapel, I went up and introduced myself. As we talked, I explained that I too was a Christian who wanted to go into the ministry. David Nicholas, the director of admissions at Los Angeles Baptist College and Seminary, stunned me by asking, "How would you like to go to Los Angeles Baptist College?"

Soon after, a letter and scholarship offer came from the basketball coach. Everything I ever wanted was suddenly within my grasp: a complete college education, paid for by a basketball scholarship, training in the Bible in preparation for ministry; a school that accepted blacks as well as whites; and most of all, a chance to finally get free of Mississippi. Why, then, was I afraid?

Fortunately, I wasn't alone in the situation. My buddy Jimmy Walker was given the same offer.

All the self-doubt, fear, and inferiority that we'd grown up with were lashing us with a fury, beating us down. It was as if the entire weight of the system was fighting against us in an all-out effort to keep us forever chained in hopelessness.

Suddenly, I realized that the only thing standing in my way was me. Finally, I resolved to go for it, and I turned to Jimmy and said, "I'll go if you'll go!" So we did.

When Jimmy and I arrived at Los Angeles Baptist College in August of 1967, our new basketball coach welcomed us with a tour of the campus. "So, Coach," I finally asked, "where are some of the other black students?"

He looked kind of funny and then said, "Well, there aren't any others. You two are the first to live on campus and go to school here." Then he piped up and said, "Uh, there's something else you need to know. You guys won't be rooming together."

Jimmy and I ditched our stuff in our respective rooms and walked off campus to see the town of Newhall. About thirty miles north of L.A. near the San Fernando Valley, the town had about fourteen thousand people. Walking through the town we soon realized there were fourteen thousand *white* people. Not only were we the only blacks at LABC—we were the only black people in town. Finally, we just had to laugh.

Still, the racial climate was very different from Simpson County. Somehow we didn't feel like second-class citizens, mostly because no one seemed to treat us that way. It gave us some hope.

In a way we walked a tightrope, trying to mix in, yet trying to remain distinctive. We decided that our main goal was to get an education, and we didn't want to interfere with that, least of all because of our race. So we put up with some inconvenience.

Often, I stopped on the steps of my dormitory and looked out at the hills surrounding Newhall. They were dry and brown and hot and dusty! I suddenly caught myself longing for the cool green fields and woods of Mississippi. I was in a strange place. I was alone. And I was downright scared. I was already homesick. I just kept thinking, *Man, what have I done? What in the world am I doing here?*

At my graduation, Mama was in the crowd, surrounded by the most

whites she'd ever seen at one time. The trip to California and the commencement were a highlight in her life. I think she knew, more than
anyone else, what graduating from LABC meant for me. I'd already
been accepted at the Los Angeles Baptist Seminary and would coach
the freshman basketball team at LABC. I had also met my future wife,
Rosie, a student at the college from Mississippi. I was amazed to learn
that she had left home for California with only nine dollars in her
pocket!

The decision to return to Mendenhall was six weeks in the making. I don't know when I crossed the line. I just remember that when
I came home from a mission trip to the Orient, the question was not
whether I would return, but when. In the spring after graduation from
the seminary, I did what I swore I'd never do: I moved with my new
bride back to Mississippi, to begin my ministry back where it all began.
There was little to cheer about: John Perkins had moved up to Jackson.
The only programs operating were after-school tutoring and a radio
ministry. The gains of the civil rights movement were trickling down
slowly to rural areas like Simpson County.

Was this really where God wanted me? I thought back to the tour
of the Orient, back to where I had considered taking the offer to begin
a ministry in Taiwan. A voice kept telling me, "Dolphus, I have something for you to do in Mississippi."

Rosie and I came home to Mendenhall in 1971, and we ain't never
looked back.

Alice Jackson

Alice Jackson is a veteran journalist, reporting on crime, politics, and public corruption for newspapers, television, and magazines, including *Time*, *People*, and the *New York Times*. During more than thirty years of news assignments, she has traveled the width and length of her adopted state. She resided on the shores of the Mississippi Sound outside Ocean Springs until Hurricane Katrina destroyed her home on August 29, 2005. She now works at the University of South Alabama in Mobile where she is also pursuing a master's degree in creative writing.

Katrina, a nasty divorce, and the need for a job pushed me out of Mississippi years after I adopted it as my home. The divorce, like the marriage, isn't worth discussing. I survived it. Enough said.

Still, I do wish the divorce hadn't occurred during the same time I lost my beachfront home to Katrina. Couple that with the loss of my mother's home, add the devastation of my brother and sister-in-law's house, and if you are inclined to self-pity, you have a full-blown tragedy of Greek proportions. Fortunately, I dislike self-pity as much as I dislike talking about my former marriage. As with the divorce, we all lived through Katrina, and after two years of fighting State Farm Insurance with the vengeance of a bull shark, we all got paid, which is more than many of my Gulf Coast neighbors can say.

The real tragedy was having to move away from Mississippi. The day I followed my moving van across the state line into Alabama, where I'd been fortunate enough to find work at the University of South Alabama in Mobile, I fought back tears.

A scholarship to Mississippi University for Women in Columbus, at that time one of the last two state-supported colleges for women in the nation, sparked my love affair with the state. The two things I knew about Mississippi were that William Faulkner of Oxford had won a Nobel Prize for Literature and that Willie Morris, the author of a book I admired called *North Toward Home*, was from Yazoo City. There were authors from my home state of Alabama, but in my young mind Faulkner and Morris outshone them all.

I arrived during the fall of 1971, a bespectacled and shy honor student whose head was always buried in a book. An only daughter with two older brothers, I lacked female soul mates, something the W supplied in spades. I learned about sophisticated girls, popular girls, bad girls, and, best of all, really smart, witty, and fun girls. My circle was the latter. We didn't have as many dates as the other girls, but for us life on campus was like a Walt Disney movie, specifically *The Trouble with Angels*. We were hilarious, dreaming up weekend pranks that still send us into gales of laughter when we talk. Yet, we were so innocent that the first time we sneaked alcohol into our dorm, we bathed and changed into our pajamas in preparation for the horror of passing out after one or two drinks. Like Boy Scouts, a W girl was always prepared.

The one thing I envied about my Mississippi friends was the way they connected the dots between cities and towns. If a girl from Natchez met a girl from Gulfport, they kept comparing notes for hours until they found mutual friends. Once that connection was made, they became friends for life, enlarging the great network that was Mississippi.

I'd arrived at the W with the dream to be a doctor in a time when few women even made it into medical school. Like me, the women's movement was young. Also like me, it faced a lot of struggles before things got better. By the end of my sophomore year, math had ended my medical dreams, sending me searching for another career choice where I could bury myself passionately in my work. If you didn't love your work, I believed, how could you survive the tediousness of doing it every day for years? My answer came from the travails of Richard

Nixon, the two journalists at the *Washington Post* who helped to end his presidency, and an English professor who scrawled a note on one of my essays. "In all my years of teaching, I've never seen a young student write about life with so much compassion and earnestness," she said. "You should think about a career that involves writing."

Armed with a journalism degree and intent on changing the world, I landed my first job at the *Magee Courier*, a weekly newspaper in Simpson County. In those days, women journalists who covered big stories at big-city dailies were almost as sparse as female doctors, and rural Mississippi was a good proving ground for news cubs who needed to pay their dues before hoping to move to a bigger newspaper. Under the direction of owners Betty and Tom Dickson, I was the *Courier's* photographer and darkroom person, reporter, news editor, layout person, and third hand on the press when it cranked up each Wednesday afternoon. I didn't put any politicians in jail, but I learned how to cut hay, how to pull the best watermelon in a field, and how to make a decent strawberry pie; I discovered you don't stay too long inside chicken sheds in June, followed the city's fire trucks to every house and brush fire, and, most importantly, learned never to be curious enough at an automobile accident to look beneath the tarp spread over a dead body. And, while I thought I was learning to be a journalist, I was really being initiated into one of the most elite of southern fraternities. My network was smaller than those of my W chums, but I was slowly becoming a Mississippian.

After my eighteen months at the *Courier*, Pic Firmin, who earned his news chops under the legendary Hodding Carter, Sr., at the *Delta Democrat Times* in Greenville, hired me for a daily reporting job at the *Sun Herald* in Biloxi, and in my mind the man-made beaches of the Mississippi Gulf Coast would be my last stop before I headed for Atlanta, or maybe even farther north. It was the late 1970s, and my first beat was the environment, including the fishing and shrimping industries. In time, I learned to shrimp, fish, and crab. Later, I learned to sail and spent some of the happiest times of my life on Horn and Petit Bois islands where raccoons waddled down to the shoreline in broad daylight to wash their food in the surf before nibbling it. I marveled at "lightning in the water" during nights on Horn Island and learned to steer for Biloxi's ship channel by the lights of waterfront landmarks on U.S. 90. Over time, I stopped dreaming of moving anywhere else because life was too good where I was.

For more than thirty years I covered the best and worst of humanity in a single place bordered by I-10 to the north and the barrier islands to the south, a microcosm of the good and evil better known in much bigger cities. Sheriffs who corrupted their own departments with drug deals. Crime kingpins who killed their competitors, then stuffed the body into the trunk of the victim's own car. Lawyers who contracted to kill their best friends. Trusted politicians who betrayed their constituents for millions of dollars. I learned about strip joints, including the people who owned them and the people whose lives revolved around them. And I learned how difficult it is to convince good and decent Mississippians that one of their own, a politician who was maybe even a member of their personal network, smiled at them while robbing them behind their backs.

Near sundown on August 29, 2005, I picked my way through the debris of houses, downed trees, and destroyed cars, heading for my place on Seacliff Boulevard, east of Ocean Springs. About a block away, I met a barefoot woman, eyes red and swollen from crying. Katrina's last winds fought to steal her words.

"Don't go down there near the beach," she warned. "It's total devastation."

It was and it wasn't. My street was stripped almost bare. What the hurricane winds left behind, the tidal surge had swept away. What was left was almost unrecognizable. A piece of washing machine here. Pieces of clothing hanging from the trees there. Standing on the concrete slab where my mother's house had been were my good neighbors Don and Martha Wade, surveying the remains of their two-story home across the street. Like me and my family, they had lost everything, but we were alive. As the three of us talked, trying to accept the destruction of our lives, the sun popped out from between Katrina's final clouds, casting light diamonds across the Mississippi Sound. Months later, as I put Katrina's nightmare into focus, that scene came back to me. I had nothing left. Yet, I still had the things I cared about the most, the people close to me and the land and the water I loved.

Sometimes, I wonder if heaven means we'll get to pick our place to be, setting the scene from a perfect time in our life. If so, mine will be the night before the opening day of shrimp season when the lights of hundreds of trawlers twinkle across the Mississippi Sound from east to west, their hulls so close together a person could walk from Alabama to Louisiana across the decks as the drone of their engines rolls across Horn Island where I stand on sands lit by the Milky Way's canopy, happy to be home.

Kevin Bullard

Colonel Kevin Lee Bullard, a native Jacksonian, grew up in Magee and began his college career at the University of Southern Mississippi, graduating from Mississippi College in 1990. He joined the Mississippi National Guard in January of 1983 and was commissioned a second lieutenant in June of 1988. He was mobilized in support of Operation Desert Storm in 1991 and spent six months at Fort Lewis, Washington. Later, he was deployed to Afghanistan. In 2012, he was promoted to colonel, and he currently works full time for the Mississippi National Guard. He and his wife, Tamara, and son, Peyton, live in Madison.

It was 1983. I had just finished my first semester at the University of Southern Mississippi and was trying to figure out how to pay for my second. Though I didn't know anybody in the National Guard, when I drove past the armory in Magee, my hometown at the time, the idea struck me that they could somehow help me pay for school. Nowhere in my eighteen-year-old mind did I imagine that twenty-eight years later, I'd still be in, that I'd be a lieutenant colonel or, least of all, that I would be in Afghanistan. I had mobilized for Desert Storm in 1991, but served stateside in Fort Lewis, Washington. For whatever reason, I honestly didn't think I would get called up for Operation Iraqi Freedom or Operation Enduring Freedom. I'd never tried to get out of going; I just felt like I hadn't been needed. I did raise my right hand and swear an oath that I take very seriously, to support and defend. So, when I received notification that I was being transferred to a deploying unit, I didn't complain. I was glad to do my part.

For all practical purposes, we, the 184th Expeditionary Sustainment Command, mobilized on the seventh day of June 2010. Even though we weren't technically on active duty, we only had a couple of weeks at home between then and our departure to Afghanistan the first week of October. We spent several weeks at Fort Lee, Virginia, several at Camp Shelby, Mississippi, and finally a couple of months at Fort Hood, Texas, before heading overseas.

I can't say I hadn't been warned about the conditions at Kandahar Airfield (a.k.a. KAF), but I will say that all the talk, all the briefings and all the photos didn't do it justice. We landed late at night. Even though it was early October, it was hot. The C-17 engines and the thick concrete didn't help matters, but even beyond all that, it was still very hot. Mississippi has been home all my life. I know hot. This was hot. Honestly though, the heat was much more tolerable than the thick dust in the air. Everything was covered with dust. There are probably no more than a dozen trees on the entire base, and they are almost white with dust. Greenery is rare. Shrubs, bushes, and grass are all but nonexistent. I think everything I owned there at some point was covered with dust. The heat and dust were less than pleasant, but KAF is probably best known and most remembered for its smell. Words can't adequately describe it. The odor and smoke of the burn piles and barrels is constant. What exactly is burning? For the most part, I honestly don't know. What I do know is that I missed breathing clean air terribly. Next, imagine a sewer treatment site the size of a football field, operating (or trying to operate) at several times its maximum capacity. There you have what is commonly known as the "poo pond," or sometimes simply the "pond." It's everything you would expect it to be and more. No matter where you are on KAF, when the wind is right, the experience is literally breathtaking. Suffice it to say that over those ten months, I grew to deeply appreciate clean Mississippi air, humidity and all.

Another hot topic among those spending time at KAF is the food. Generally, throughout my life, I've avoided eating things I can't easily pronounce or readily identify. That didn't work there. I gladly admit that over the last several months of my deployment, the food got much, much better. For the most part, even though my standards aren't what they used to be, I'd say it was good. But prior to about the end of March, such was not the case. At the risk of sounding like a complainer, I will say that had it not been for the generous people back home sending care packages filled with food, I would have skipped quite a few meals. I will, however, give the dining facilities credit; the food was both hot and plentiful. I'd been in country for over seven months before my turn rolled around for R&R—my chance to spend two weeks at home. By the time I was ready, I actually had a list of food I wanted to eat. Of course, some of my favorite home-cooked meals topped the list. Fried shrimp, beef stroganoff, and chicken and broccoli casserole were on the list and I enjoyed all three. Among the dining-out favorites that were calling to me were a juicy Five Guys burger, an AJ's beef filet topped with crabmeat, and a Beagle Bagel chicken salad on panini. I had all three of those.

On a more serious note, KAF is a fairly dangerous place. Indirect fire (IDF) attacks were not uncommon. I believe it is purely God's hand of protection that caused the enemies' poor aim with their rockets. Otherwise, many more lives would have been lost. There's not much more I can say about that with combat operations still ongoing. I can say I have felt the ground shake on more occasions than I care to remember. I can say I missed a peaceful shower without wondering in the back of my mind if it would be interrupted by explosions and alarms. Make no mistake, I don't take for granted the men and women risking their lives outside the wire every day in convoys and other missions. The danger on KAF pales in comparison, but it is still something to be taken seriously.

I am not bothered by the sound of the alarm or the explosions. I don't think those thoughts will follow me. What I am bothered by is the memory of a flag-covered metal box with a nineteen-year-old army private first class from New York inside, or the twenty-two-year-old marine lance corporal from California; the list goes on. I am bothered by the memory of the flag at half-mast so much of the time. I will never forget the emotional ceremonies as "Taps" was played to honor our fallen heroes before they were flown back to the United States. I will never forget the lump in my throat as I rendered the ceremonial hand salute for those who gave their all. I have always considered myself a patriot. For as long as I can remember, the playing of the national anthem has given me goose bumps. And now I hear it with a whole new perspective.

It's only natural that we sometimes take things for granted until we don't have them anymore. I missed a hot bath, good seafood, and the sound of my dogs barking. I missed riding my bike on the Natchez Trace. I missed the smell of freshly cut grass and the view of the Ross Barnett Reservoir as I drove across the spillway. I missed Smoothie King and Dairy Queen and Millie D's, the new yogurt place down the road from my house. I missed the smell of my truck and the fresh wind in my face as I drove with the windows down. I longed to see my sister and brothers, nieces and nephews, aunts, uncles, cousins, and in-laws. I was ready to see my church family from Colonial Heights Baptist, my friends at work, and my instructors and fellow students at Griffin's TaeKwonDo Academy. Most of all, I yearned to hold my wife and spend time with my son. There's no doubt that being apart from my family was the hardest thing throughout the whole deployment. The time apart gave me a new appreciation for them.

As a general rule, time goes by very fast during a deployment. Working thirteen-to-fifteen-hour days, six and a half days a week doesn't leave much downtime to drag by. Up at 5:30 a.m. and off to work, back around 8:30 p.m., shower and bed. Get up the next day and do it again. We call it "Groundhog Day," but it does make the time seem to pass quickly. It's those last few days, when the mission is complete and we're just waiting on the trip home, that seem to drag. Days seem like weeks.

I left Kandahar on the evening of July 26. I have to say that was a great day. I knew the trip itself would be less than fun. It's simply not possible to get from that side of the world to this one without losing at least one entire night's sleep. Of course, the end result makes it all worthwhile. After two nights at Manas Airbase in Kyrgyzstan, and a few hours in Shannon, Ireland, we were on our way to the United States. The final layover in Bangor, Maine, is an experience in itself.

Whether heading off to the war or coming home from it, units are greeted by a host of people. My guess is that those good people don't miss an opportunity for hugs, handshakes, and well wishes. It is truly emotional and inspiring. Our plane touched down in Gulfport, Mississippi, on the afternoon of July 29, which also happened to be my twenty-second wedding anniversary. A short bus ride north to Camp Shelby and I received the best anniversary gift I could possibly ask for, the open arms of my family. I didn't want to let go of my wife, Tamara, and my son, Peyton. It seemed almost too good to be real. There were literally hundreds of people at Camp Shelby to greet us. Four nights there, and I was finally on my way to my home in Madison. As I turned into my subdivision, I passed welcome home signs and a yard full of flags in front of my house. The freshly cut grass, the new pine straw in the flowerbeds, and the blooms on the crepe myrtles were a sight to behold. Those things don't seem like much in the normal day-to-day, but after a year of looking at dust and dodging rockets, I found them worth getting excited over. Since coming home, I've made several trips to Millie D's, enjoyed a Mississippi Braves baseball game, and had too much good food to eat. I've spent hours and hours with my wife and son. This morning, with the temperature a pleasant seventy-one degrees, I took the time for a two-mile run around our lake and a ten-mile bike ride down the Highland Colony Parkway and the trails by the Natchez Trace. The clean air and clear blue skies made me want to spend all day outside. I will never again take for granted this wonderful state of Mississippi. I can truly say it's great to come home.

Curtis Wilkie

Curtis Wilkie was born in Mississippi and spent most of the early part
his life in the state. After beginning his career as a journalist with the
Clarksdale Press Register, he went on to become a national and foreign
correspondent for the *Boston Globe*, where he worked for more than
a quarter-century. He is the author of three books: *Arkansas Mischief*,
Dixie, and *The Fall of the House of Zeus*. He now lives with his wife,
Nancy, in Oxford, where he teaches journalism at Ole Miss and serves
as a fellow at the Overby Center for Southern Journalism and Politics.

Home is not just where the heart is; it's the place where we feel most
comfortable.

In a lifetime filled with many moves and much upheaval, I spent
years in four different cities that I loved: Washington, Boston, Jerusalem, and New Orleans. Though I called each place "home," at one
time or another, I had a nagging sense that I never quite fit in any of
them. I lacked childhood memories of classroom chums and youthful
adventures in their territory. I had no family legacy in societies where
that sort of thing counted, no personal standing, no parish to call my
own. My Mississippi accent sounded foreign to local ears, even in New
Orleans, with its special patois, and language created a barrier for me
overseas.

As much as I wanted to belong in these cities, I dwelled in them as
an outsider.

My desire to be a part of a place might be traced to my peripatetic
childhood, when I lived in no less than eleven locations in my first

135

seven years. The names and the nostalgia retained from that period are a blur: Greenville, Memphis, Knoxville, Oak Ridge, El Paso, Oxford, a town in west Tennessee whose name is lost to me, Oxford (again), Sardis, the Ole Miss campus while my mother earned a master's degree, and, finally, the little south Mississippi community of Summit, where my mother and I settled in 1947.

Although we had no family connections there, Summit became the first place where I felt grounded—albeit in a strange environment. We lived in the girls' dormitory at Southwest Mississippi Junior College where my mother, a widow, was dean of women and registrar, taught psychology and English, and had other roles. I joined a pack of faculty children; we were known as the "campus brats." Because there seemed to be no threat of another imminent disruption in our lives, I enjoyed a feeling of stability. And then, when the move occurred, it was a good one. My mother married the local Presbyterian minister, and we simply took ourselves a mile into town.

Summit lay on two of the principal routes in Mississippi at the time: the main line of the Illinois Central Railroad and U.S. Highway 51. It was a lumber and railroad town, cheek-to-jowl with bigger McComb. A few more than a thousand people lived there, and Summit gave every impression of being "sleepy"—a cliché travel writers use to describe small southern towns. I had my own perspective, though, as I wrote decades later in *Dixie*, my book about the transformation of the South: "From the window of a train, blowing past in a wink, the place looked no different from any other town along the way. But Summit's population was full of eccentrics, artists, romantics, more than its share of closet alcoholics, as well as a bona fide village idiot, and it seemed to me enchanted. . . ."

We lived there for nine years of small-town bliss. We never locked doors. I bicycled to school. I developed close friendships and played—though never very well—football, basketball, and baseball. I felt a fixture there. Then, in the midst of my sophomore year in high school, we were uprooted. My stepfather accepted a ministry more than three hundred miles away, in Corinth, and I never really made the emotional transition. As a teenager, I found it hard to adjust to a new setting. I consoled myself by identifying with the James Dean character thrown into a new high school in the movie *Rebel Without a Cause*. I went so far as to buy a red nylon jacket, similar to the one Dean wore, and when I flirted with trouble in Corinth I may have been unconsciously emulating the role of the doomed, romantic actor.

In the fall of 1958, I went off to Ole Miss at the same time my stepfather was recalled to the church in Summit. My parents were gloriously happy to return to the "enchanted" village and spent the rest of their lives there. When I visit their graves in the Summit cemetery, I feel as though I am among friends. So many townspeople that I knew, my elders as well as my contemporaries, are buried there. If asked, over the years, where was "home," I instinctively answered: a little town in south Mississippi called Summit. But it has been more than fifty years—with many stops—since I lived there.

After college, I returned to the Delta, where I was born, to work in Clarksdale. In those days, the landed gentry ruled the region. I was never part of that class. As a result of my role as a newspaper reporter, I was probably considered an "outside agitator." I wrote obits and book reviews, covered civic clubs, cops, and city hall, and ranged a bit around the state on the political beat. But the biggest story, day in and day out, was the civil rights movement, and as I wrote about the struggle I alienated a lot of people. Troubled, myself, by the hold that the old Confederacy had on Mississippi, a reactionary mentality that branded any new idea as a communist plot, I began to look for relief. I read Willie Morris's memoir, *North Toward Home*, and envied his flight from Yazoo City to New York. I, too, wanted to move to the East Coast, to become part of a group Morris described as "a genuine set of exiles, almost in the European sense: alienated from home yet forever drawn back to it, seeking some form of personal liberty elsewhere yet obsessed with the texture and the complexity of the place from which they had departed as few Americans from other states could ever be."

I got my wish, a Congressional Fellowship, and went to Washington, where I would eventually spend more than ten years during two separate stays. For all of the complaints about "Washington"—a catchword for an unresponsive federal bureaucracy and unpopular

government policies—it is a lovely city, unburdened by an old aris-
tocracy. Constant political turnover ensures change. It's a place where
transients can quickly find niches. It's neither north nor south. With its
immense concentration of journalists, I made many friends there. But
somehow, it was never quite home.

Boston appealed to me, if for no other reason, because Massachusetts had been the only state that George McGovern carried over Richard Nixon in 1972. Despite the city's long history, its many universities
gave Boston a youthful vibrancy as well as intellectual firepower. But I
landed there in the midst of the school integration–busing crisis and
discovered that racism was not an exclusively southern characteristic.
The city was divided into about twenty neighborhoods where the in-
habitants were as turf-conscious as the tribal combatants of Lebanon.
Having driven the Protestants to the suburbs earlier in the twentieth
century, the Irish majority wrestled for supremacy with a growing Ital-
ian-American population, and neither side wanted to cede anything to
blacks or Hispanics. I lived in a neighborhood as Irish as Dublin, but
the fact that my ancestors came from Ireland did me no good there. My
accent betrayed me as a southerner, and many Bostonians harbored a
condescension for things southern.

My job pushed me to Jerusalem. The tone for my life there was set
in a taxi ride to Kennedy Airport to catch a flight to Israel. As I con-
versed with the New York cab driver, telling him of my destination,
he eyed me suspiciously in the mirror. "Ya don't look Jewish to me," he
remarked. I had a marvelous experience in the Middle East. Lots of
great stories to cover, a ton of interesting people. But I knew I was far
from home.

After spending several years abroad and a second tour of duty in
Boston, I pondered yet another move. Willie Morris, by this time my
friend, encouraged me to "come home." He said I should write my own
book about my exodus—and the lure to return to our native region—
and call it "South to New Orleans."

Growing up, I had been fascinated with nearby New Orleans,
dreaming of one day living in the French Quarter. In 1993, with my

mother gravely ill in Summit, I bought a pied-à-terre on Gov. Nicholls Street with a balcony looking toward Jackson Square and the river. I was my mother's only close relative, and the New Orleans location facilitated my visits to her bedside.

On one trip south, I went with my Jackson friends, Pat and Butch Cothren, to a game in Oxford, my first Ole Miss football experience in twenty-five years. More gratifying than the victory over Georgia was the Grove. The stately old grounds I remembered from my childhood and student days had been turned into a spectacle, almost psychedelic in its colors and procession of long-lost classmates. Two days later, I would appeal to my editors in Boston to allow me to spend the coming winter in New Orleans, to use the South as a base for my assignments as a national reporter. They agreed. I promised to return to Boston in the spring. I lied.

Washed in the warmth of a New Orleans winter, I was delighted to be within walking distance of two of my favorite spots, the Napoleon House and Galatoire's. Once the fairgrounds was rebuilt after a fire, my affection for thoroughbred racing was rekindled. New Orleans was a place where I had ancient memories: of baseball games at Pelican Stadium and matinees at the Saenger Theatre; of being dragged by Mother on shopping expeditions to Maison Blanche; of rowdy evenings as a college student slumming in the raunchy Latin bar on the Decatur Street waterfront known as La Casa.

I felt that I fit in there. At least in the French Quarter. But I found New Orleans a Balkanized city where the French Quarter represented an aberration with only three thousand citizens. The city's real heart lay in its growing black neighborhoods and its old, white working-class wards, while financial power resided "Uptown," where superiority seemed to ooze from the mansions along the St. Charles streetcar line. I would never feel a part of those places.

Yet things have a way of falling into place late in life.

My daughter, Leighton, and her husband, Campbell McCool, actually led my way back to Oxford. In 1997, they bought a second home, a cottage on South Eleventh Street, a few blocks from the square. We began to spend football weekends there, and they graciously let me use it for other getaways. I began to rediscover the town where my mother grew up, where I had lived as a child and a college student.

Oxford had changed dramatically. It had grown from a rural county seat to a cosmopolitan university town. Its square, where alcohol had been banned during my college days, offered restaurants with fancy wine lists and cozy bars with live music and a throbbing nightlife. There had not been a bookstore in Oxford during Faulkner's lifetime; now Square Books, one of the best independent stores in America, held down the corner where Blaylock's Drug Store once stood. Prominent writers made it a regular stop on their book tours. The town also supported a flourishing arts and music scene.

Cultural life had exploded on the campus, too: concerts featuring local talent as well as visiting orchestras, fine theatre performances, and frequent lectures by distinguished speakers.

Like so many other Ole Miss alumni from my generation who were relocating in Oxford, I found myself drawn back. After I retired from the *Boston Globe*, I bought that South Eleventh Street cottage while Leighton and Campbell—who has roots in Oxford, too—wound up building their principal residence next door.

We were in the vanguard of the large migration to Oxford that began at the end of the twentieth century. I didn't feel like a newcomer. I'm not sure I qualify as "old Oxford," but the town has been home to my mother's side of my family for nearly a hundred years, so that should give me some cachet.

There is something comforting about Oxford. To pass the home where my grandparents lived; it still stands on Van Buren Avenue, two blocks from the square. To drive by the cemetery where so many of my relatives lie under its gentle hills. To use the same sidewalks I traversed as a child on the way to movies at the Lyric or Ritz theatres. To be back in the company of my first cousin, Bob Black (we are the same age and he has long served as the brother I never had) and other friends from Ole Miss days.

I became a part of the university community again, joining the journalism faculty at Ole Miss. I enjoyed special pleasures—not only teaching feature writing, a course I had failed in 1961 for turning in assignments late, but having lunch from time to time with Jere Hoar, the professor who flunked me.

In 2007, I married Nancy, a delightfully vivacious woman I remembered from my Clarksdale days when she was an Ole Miss girl from the Delta. To join me, she moved from Memphis where she had lived for years. One of her sons wondered about her departure from the city and asked, "What will you do in Oxford?" Nancy laughs about that when we head off to yet another event, another engagement with friends, another Ole Miss game. Her sister, Melissa, who lives in New York, thinks Nancy sees more interesting people in Oxford than she does in Manhattan.

Our lot on South Eleventh is deep and easily accommodated expansion when we doubled the square footage of the cottage. We have a dog and a cat and a host of local friends. In fair weather, we sit on our screened back porch, listening to the Ole Miss band rehearsing in the distance or to the sounds of my grandsons cavorting in the pool next door. Timorous game—deer, rabbits, a curious groundhog—occasionally approach our backyard from the woods at the foot of our land.

Oxford seems incredibly serene. Nancy and I believe we have come happily full circle. And, at last, I feel that I have come home.

Tricia Walker

Tricia Walker, award-winning songwriter and recording artist, is the director of the Delta Music Institute, a recording arts and music industry
studies program at her alma mater Delta State University. Walker spent
twenty-six years in Nashville, where her songs were recorded by a number of artists including Faith Hill, Patty Loveless, and Alison Krauss,
whose performance of Tricia's "Looking in the Eyes of Love" earned a
Grammy. Tricia's CD, *The Heart of Dixie*, captures the songwriter's view
of the South with lyrics and music that reflect her folk, R & B, and
storytelling influences. Before moving to Nashville in the 1980s, Tricia
earned a degree in music education from Delta State University and a
master of music degree from Mississippi College. For more information,
contact www.bigfrontporch.com.

A s I write this, I am riding north on the City of New Orleans train
headed back to the Mississippi Delta. The gentle rhythm of the
rails as we move along evokes an early comfortable memory of
traveling which foreshadowed much of my professional life. And now,
it seems, the roads I've traveled have come full circle to bring me home
to Mississippi.

I was raised in Jefferson County, just north of the county seat of
Fayette, in an antebellum house in which Jefferson Davis is reported
to have been the home's first overnight guest. I had what felt like a
carefree childhood, growing up a tomboy, riding my horse through
the woods and pastures, fancying myself as Roy Rogers or Zorro. My
earliest musical memories came from learning songs in Sunday school

at the Methodist Church, hearing my mama and daddy's big band records on the stereo, and listening to a Tchaikovsky classical record that my mama brought home from the grocery store after redeeming her green stamps. But my lifelong love of learning about music began when I started taking piano lessons at the age of six from Mrs. Iska Montgomery. She was the school's music teacher and had already educated the generation before me. She taught me piano through my high school years, and next to my parents, she was my greatest influence.

When I saw the Beatles on the *Ed Sullivan Show* on a Sunday night in 1964, my course was set. I soon became the proud owner of a thirty-five-dollar Kay acoustic guitar from the local Western Auto store. After I was able to successfully form an F chord without shedding any blood or causing any finger "buzz," I knew I could conquer any song in my path. My first band was named the Mishaps, a fierce four-piece combo that played hits from the Monkees to Jimi Hendrix to Wilson Pickett at Saturday night dances at the local American Legion hut. Because my father was involved in state politics, we had the opportunity to hit the campaign trail one summer for a memorable string of political engagements. It was my first tour. I was fourteen. The Mishaps and AM radio formed my pop and rock education, but I learned the acoustic side of music and three-part harmony singing with my two best friends. We must have performed at least twice in every church of every denomination in southwest Mississippi.

I never had a senior year of high school. The racial tension from all the social change going on in Mississippi, and Fayette in particular, and the desegregation of the public schools made for a tense learning environment, so I finished a year early and headed to Copiah-Lincoln Community College with my two best friends. But the seeds of the issues of race, faith, and reconciliation began to take root as a basis for my future musical work. I began to write what looked like songs during my early college years, and after I earned a bachelor of music education degree from Delta State University, I moved back to the Jackson area to begin work on a graduate degree. In between singing covers three to four nights a week in Jackson venues and doing my graduate work, I entered a few of my original songs in the Mississippi and

American Song Festivals and won prizes in two categories. The professional musicians that I knew in Jackson suggested that if I were going to try the music business for real I would need to move to New York, Los Angeles, or Nashville. Fayette was a town of sixteen hundred, so for a small-town southern girl, New York felt too big and LA seemed too far away, so Nashville looked like the option for me, even though all I knew about country music was seeing a few episodes of Porter Wagoner's Saturday afternoon television show. But Nashville was five hundred miles from Fayette, so I knew that if the music biz didn't work out, I could get home pretty quickly. One thing that pounded in my head for sure was that the fear of failing was not nearly as strong as the fear of not trying. So on a hot sultry August afternoon, I loaded a U-Haul and left my dear Mississippi for Music City—Nashville, Tennessee.

My career in Music City was a magical one. I had opportunities to be a backing musician for Opry great Connie Smith, Mississippi native Paul Overstreet, and pop/country star Shania Twain. I wrote for two major publishing companies. I met Faith Hill when she was a receptionist and she later recorded one of my songs and performed it on the CMA Awards show. Roy Acuff visited my home and gave an impromptu performance of "Wabash Cannonball" on my back porch. I performed before a Farm Aid audience of over forty thousand and traveled to Europe, Canada, and New Zealand. The Women in The Round songwriter group, made up of award-winning singer/songwriters Ashley Cleveland, Pam Tillis, Karen Staley, and myself, became a fixture at the Bluebird Cafe for over twenty years. Alison Krauss won a Grammy™ award for her performance of one of my songs. I ran an independent publishing company and performed in my own group, the Mudcats, for over ten years. I sang for Robert Redford at his Christmas party and watched the Nashville Ballet choreograph dances to my songs. Lifelong friends I made in Nashville saw me through the best of times and through the darkest of times, and they all knew that, although I lived in Tennessee, I was *from* Mississippi.

At the end of the millennium, I began to teach a couple of songwriting courses at Nashville State Community College, which is where I first heard of a plan to start a music industry program at Delta State. I didn't think a lot about it at the time, but on my way home to Mississippi for Christmas one year, I stopped by the campus to meet Norbert Putnam, the director of the new Delta Music Institute program. I filed away a thought that perhaps I could teach my songwriting course at DSU someday, and then I turned my focus back to my work on a multimedia songwriter show called *The Heart of Dixie*, built around the themes of race and reconciliation.

In late August of 2005, my two best friends, my sister, and I gathered for our annual summer get-together on the Mississippi Gulf Coast. We leisurely watched weather updates as a storm named Katrina first came across Florida as a Category 1 hurricane. The following day, when it became apparent Katrina was re-forming in the gulf and headed for the coast, we packed our friend's house up as best we could, and I started back to Nashville with a troubled heart. Over the following days, I watched in horror as Katrina broke the Mississippi coast into a million jagged pieces. It was almost too much to bear. Later that fall, with my heart still aching, I recall thinking, "What would it be like to go back home to Mississippi?" I spoke the thought out loud at Christmas to my two best friends and they were both overjoyed. I spoke the thought out loud to my Nashville friends after the first of the year, and although they were sad, they all affirmed that it was time for me to "go home." But how would I live? Music City had given me multiple opportunities to touch every part of the music industry, to be an entrepreneurial, self-supporting writer/artist/producer/publisher, and to be able to work every day doing what I love to do. Music City had the environment to make that kind of life possible. But how could I do that in Mississippi? My decision to "come home" was set. I was at peace about that, but unsure as to what the day-to-day would look like.

In the spring of 2006, a call came from my alma mater, Delta State University, saying that the music industry program was going forward, but the director, Mr. Putnam, was leaving the position. The dean asked if I would be interested in applying. No bells rang. There was no bolt of lightning. It was as if a curtain was slowly parting, revealing the next act of the play I was watching on stage. It was a slow turning and it made sense. All that I had learned in almost thirty years as a music industry professional could be put into play to help prepare and educate the next generation of young Mississippi musicians, songwriters, and engineers about the music industry. Oddly enough (or maybe not so odd), when I read back through my journals I found references and thoughts about coming home as far back as eight or ten years before I returned. I suppose it was meant to be all along . . . just a matter of when.

As circles are created to do, they come back around to where they started. And so on another sultry summer day, I loaded another moving truck and headed back to my beloved Mississippi to say "yes" to a unique opportunity with DSU and the music industry studies program of the Delta Music Institute. To say I am grateful is an extreme understatement, and for as much time as I've spent with the road moving under my feet and the hum of the highway in my ears, it is good to be back in the Magnolia State . . . the birthplace of America's music . . . Mississippi . . . home.

Sela Ward

Sela Ward, a Meridian native, attended the University of Alabama at Tuscaloosa before going to New York City where she worked as a commercial model. She later moved to Hollywood to work in TV and feature films. She has won two Emmys, a Cable Ace Award, and a Golden Globe Award for her work. She founded Hope Village for Children in Meridian to provide shelter for children in need. In 2002, she wrote her memoir entitled *Homesick*.

They say that once you marry and start a family, you start to return to your own childhood, consciously or not. And that's what happened for me, in a big way. Our wedding was in May, and by December we'd already begun digging our toes back into the southern soil.

That first summer as husband and wife, Howard and I were still living *la vida loca*, traveling a lot, eating dinner out every night, making the most of our newlywed life. But we were also in our midthirties, and the urge to make life a nonstop romantic adventure was something we'd both gotten pretty much out of our system. We were both ready to start building something solid and lasting. Before long I was telling Howard that it would be nice if we could give our kids (*Kids!* We'd been married a month!) a taste of home down South.

At first Howard just listened, a little bemused. "It was like that six-month honeymoon period new presidents have, where Congress gives them the leeway to pass new legislation," he told me recently. "I just thought, 'Sure, honey, whatever you want.' I was determined for you to think you'd married the greatest guy in the world. I didn't want you to have buyer's remorse. It seemed to me that you had this *Field of Dreams* fantasy: if we built the farm, everything else would come."

By "building the farm," what Howard meant was a dream I'd been quietly cultivating for years, mostly unawares, but which now was breaking happily through to the surface. I wanted to go back to Meridian, at last. To take my husband and our children there, to expose us all to the fresh air and soil and good people of the land where I'd been raised.

I hadn't realized, until I was married, how powerful this impulse within me had grown to be. But I know that for years I had always loved the idea of a family compound—not so much a lavish, Kennedy-style family seat, but a decent parcel of land where my family could gather and enjoy the countryside together. I'd grown tired of vacation spots; I wanted not just a place to get away from it all, but a place that was a destination all its own. I'd been to the home of one of Berry's friends, whose family had a kind of enclave in the country outside of Meridian; I remembered our riding horses down a dirt road there, under the canopy of oak trees, and just thinking, *This is perfect*. And that image stayed with me long enough that eventually I realized it wasn't just an idle whim—it was something I needed.

"What I didn't know was that once we found a place, you'd want to go there every time you had ten minutes away from work," Howard says, laughing. "If I'd known we'd be spending 80 percent of our vacations in one spot, I might have suggested a flat in Paris."

But he never got the chance. Right away I enlisted Daddy's help as a land scout, and before we knew it he'd found the perfect tract of land, a hilly spread that had once been a dairy farm. "This real estate man showed me all over the country outside of Meridian," Daddy says. "As soon as we came upon this place, it looked like heaven, almost. The minute I saw it, I said, 'You don't have to go anywhere else, I'm going to call her and tell her I found the place.'" We call it Honeysuckle Farms.

As soon as we'd made it ours, we started planning. One ideal building site on the land was already occupied, by a dilapidated old fishing shack next to one of the ponds; the building itself wasn't really worth saving, but it had a gorgeous old redbrick chimney, and we decided to rescue it so that we could build our new home around an old hearth. Interior design is a passion of mine, so the chance to design our new cottage from scratch was a dream come true. But what kind of place did I want? It needed to be practical enough to house the family Howard and I wanted to have, but also dreamy enough to fulfill my desire for a serene country retreat, a sacred space where I could soothe my city-battered soul. I wanted this little house to feel embracing and comforting, to be not just a spare vacation cabin but a home that expressed my personality. What's more, I wanted the décor to be visibly southern, so my guests from points north and west would be swept away by the sense of place—and, for that matter, so would I.

Just as soon as we'd gotten started, of course, our wish list got away from us. We wanted a master bedroom; we wanted a suite for Mama and Daddy; we wanted a suite for Jenna to use when she came home. We wanted sleeping porches for the kids, once we had them. We wanted a gym, a study that could double as a screening room, and a great room for entertaining. But when an architect friend drew up some plans that accommodated all our wishes, we saw with astonishment that our little starter home had mushroomed to ten thousand square feet—hardly the cozy cottage of our dreams. So we shelved those plans for the time being, and decided to start small.

The design Howard and I finally settled on could hardly have been more simple. Our little shingled cottage is essentially a one-room structure, modeled after the San Ysidro Ranch cottage where we spent our honeymoon night. It's dominated by our brick hearth, with a little bathroom off the back, and a nook-size children's bedroom as well. The kitchen wraps around behind the hearth. We gave it a big screen porch, deep enough to host dinner parties on; fronted it with a creaky screen door; bookended it with porch swings; and filled it with rocking chairs looking out over the pond. And we garlanded the front with a lush, flowering English garden full of azaleas, gardenias, and roses. We southerners have always had a soft spot for all things English. At the time I was reading a romantic novel (by Rosamunde Pilcher, I think), in which the author described an English countryside manor where each bedroom was named after a different flower. I was so taken by the romance of the idea that I decided our getaway place would be called the Rose Cottage.

For the interior I cobbled together a look that was floral and feminine. I spent weekends in New Orleans buying art objects, antique furniture, and other Victoriana from auction galleries. I kept my eye out for special pieces that were historically faithful to the antebellum South. And I had some lucky finds: four-poster canopy beds and music stands to use as end tables, nineteenth-century botanical prints (roses, of course) to line the walls, and rose-shaped iron finials to crown the posts at the base of the cottage stoop. A pair of highly polished men's riding boots I fell in love with sit beside a venerable-looking writing desk, with an antique chair I found in L.A. (The dealer swore he'd bought it from Elliott Gould, and that it had belonged to him and Barbara Streisand; I guess I just needed a little taste of Hollywood, even here.)

As we finished off the inside of the cottage, we also added a few homey amenities to the grounds: hammocks and Adirondack chairs scattered about near the house, birdhouses in the trees, and a fishing pier on the pond. We even built a little island in the pond for the waterfowl, covered it with azalea bushes and a gazebo, and joined it to the bank with a white wooden arched bridge. Every evening we spent down there in those early days, we repaired to the porch to gaze out at our slice of heaven: weeping willows frame the view of the pond, and lazy ducks, swans, and geese glide on the pond till darkness falls.

Two years after we finished the Rose Cottage, we completed a second cabin nearby. Less ornamented, more rustic, this two-bedroom cottage was dubbed the Cotton Patch, after a charming country restaurant outside Tuscaloosa I'd loved during my college years. We planted a real cotton patch out front by the gravel road, and now my children love picking it and taking it back to school in Los Angeles for show-and-tell.

I still look forward to building a big house here one day; as a hopeless romantic, I think of it as my Tara. But for now we're deliriously happy in this pair of pocket-size dwellings. The Rose Cottage and the

Cotton Patch: together they're a home away from home, a sanctuary, a nurturing space where I can be still and at rest and one with the land. It took a lot of patience and introspection to pull together the elements of this physical environment, and I took no end of pleasure in the process. But it takes more than just interior decoration to make a sacred space like this. The magic I feel when we arrive at the cottages after a long stretch in the city, I think, has less to do with what Howard and I have built here physically than with what we want to build here spiritually. It takes in so many deeper wishes of mine: to carve out a safe and sane place to raise my family. To immerse us all in surroundings that are quieter, gentler, more natural and unhurried. To maintain a connection with the people I love, and the land of my raising. And above all to have a place, as Ellis Peters wrote, "where I put my feet up and thank God."

Russell Knight

Russell Knight is a master craftsman and a true pioneer of taxidermy. His thriving company, Knight's Taxidermy, is based in Anchorage, Alaska, and is the setting for his television show *Mounted in Alaska*. Born in Jackson, he is an avid outdoorsman, published author, Civil War buff, and proud conservationist. Knight also created, patented, and sold the first "fish hat," a silly idea that earned him enough money to circle the globe three times on hunting expeditions into some of the most treacherous places on the planet. He and his wife, Jerri, live in Anchorage.

I left Mississippi in a hurry and I didn't look back—for almost thirty years, that is. I grew up in Jackson, and had a strong family at home. My mother was head nurse of the emergency room at University Hospital and my dad worked for Allstate Insurance. He was an awesome piano player and had his own band. I was taught at the early age of eleven how to work for what I wanted. I mowed yards, worked at a garden center, and pumped gas at the Star gas station to make a few dollars to buy whatever I wanted, and buy is what I did. By the age of fifteen, I had bought ten-speed bicycles, canoes, and shotguns. The big ticket items were what I wanted and I wasn't afraid to work to get them!

My dad, the artist of the family, was a great mosaic tile artist. His mosaics featuring wildlife art were almost Picasso-like, but in tile. Working with my dad helped give me an eye for detail and it was this early training in drawing, composition, and tile cutting and interest in wildlife art that lead me to my ultimate career. My mom gave me her hard-driving work ethic and the gift of gab. It's this love of telling a story that has helped me over the years and I always say that I just operate in the BS mode but everything I say is mostly true! These skills helped me later in life, and eventually led to a TV show on the History Channel called *Mounted in Alaska*.

I graduated from Provine High School in 1976 and lived through the desegregation of schools, Hurricane Camille, and the oppressive heat and humidity of the South. I lived a very commonplace and stable life provided to me and my siblings by our parents, who were originally from Ellisville, Mississippi, in Jones County. My maternal grandparents, the Camps, had a small farm and struggled to survive just like everyone else, but they lived a very rich and wholesome lifestyle. Some of my fondest memories are of my grandfather and me walking around his big garden checking his strawberries and watermelons. I can remember him cutting a sugarcane stalk and us chewing sugarcane until our jaws ached! Back then, a Coke would burn your nose, there were no seatbelts in cars, and your parents let you stand on the front seat as they drove down the street.

At the age of eighteen, with a burning desire to make my own way in life, I left the state of Mississippi seeking my fame and fortune. I chose Alaska as my new home, arriving on April Fool's Day, 1977. This gigantic state they call "the Great Land" provided me adventure and a custom-tailored lifestyle built by me to suit my wants and needs perfectly. I fell in love with Alaska and for years I never even considered leaving the state. Eventually, the idea of raising my kids so far away from their grandparents was a very hard thing, as well as being thousands of miles away from all of the family.

I never forgot where I came from and for some reason my deep southern accent opened doors everywhere I went. My southern upbringing served me very well, as I met many wonderful people from all over the world. I learned that a good dose of southern kindness and hospitality works on anyone from anywhere. I kept the lessons I learned while growing up and I apply them every day of my life. When asked, I always proudly claim my Mississippi heritage and say that I'm a Mississippian, that I moved to Alaska, and now I call myself a "southern" Alaskan.

So after thirty years of raising a family and building a business through hard work, I developed a deep desire to reconnect with my roots. I decided to reach out to my long-lost friends and family in Mississippi. I returned, after all these years, bought some land on a lake, and established a small residence near Braxton, Mississippi. This allows me to have some brief reflection of my youth through fishing and hunting in the area.

Of course, things have changed, yet many things remain the same. My home in Mississippi, the one I grew up in, looks like it has been firebombed. The whole west Jackson area is a slum and has become an eyesore in the town. The west Jackson neighborhood, as I knew it, doesn't exist anymore. Yet, the Mississippi values and southern traditions are very much present and as strong as ever. Hardy Junior High School looks exactly the same as when I went there, and fried chicken, football, and saying "yes, ma'am" are still a mainstay in the Deep South. It's these things that have stood the test of time, even as other things have changed.

I think back to what it was like living in Mississippi when I was a kid. It was baseball in the summer and football in the winter. I spent every weekend with my parents helping their parents on the family farm, shelling butterbeans and peas, feeding chickens, and collecting the eggs from cranky hens I was afraid would peck me every time I reached into their nests. I can remember hanging out in the big mulberry trees, and eating purple mulberries until my stomach hurt. Pecan trees and magnolia trees are taken for granted when you live in the South; you never miss them until years later when you realize that the trees you ate from and climbed in as a kid are gone, missing from your life like an old friend you haven't seen in many years. It's these memories I have of my life, as a kid being raised in Mississippi, that have guided me through this very unusual life I have been living.

I have been fortunate in life. I found love early with my wife of thirty years, Jerri. I say I imported her in from Jackson several months after I arrived in Alaska. Together, we raised two children and built my business, Knight's Taxidermy. Life has its trials and tribulations and our family has had plenty, but together we have stood the test of time, working through the issues in life. I attribute our mutual success to a southern heritage and upbringing in a close-knit family.

I was one of a long line of Mississippians that have moved north to Alaska! For some reason Alaska had been a destination for southerners for years. One of my best friends in high school followed me up to Alaska, and as others began to show up we formed a family that we were all a part of. This support group allowed us to stay and thrive in Alaska, even though none of us had any blood relatives living close to us.

As I contemplate my future, I turn to my roots in the Deep South. I look to see if the state of Mississippi has made progress in areas that will interest my wife and me and compel us to return to the state during retirement. The wonderful community and rural towns surrounding the big city of Jackson hold many opportunities for the type of lifestyle we want to live as we grow older. The cost of living in the state is reasonable, but there are state and local sales taxes, neither of which we have in Alaska. Also, Mississippi has dry counties and you cannot buy beer on a Sunday. If you live in a dry county you'll have to travel to the next county that has a liquor store. These are just a few of the small inconveniences that are present in the South, but I say it's not all bad having some discipline these days.

Mississippi has been doing wonderful things when it comes to the wildlife management of its natural resources. When I was a young hunter in the seventies, if you saw a deer, you shot it. These days, through sound management of the whitetail deer, the Mississippi deer population is now a much sought-after resource that is a proven wildlife management success. Hunting whitetail deer lures nonresident hunters into the state, bringing much-needed revenue into Mississippi. Also, the state was wise enough to offer a nonresident native son hunting license that helps convince ex-Mississippians to come spend their money in Mississippi. It's these kinds of things that really encourage tourists, hunters, fishermen, and those native-born Mississippians from other regions to come back and enjoy what the state has to offer.

Besides the wonderful outdoors, the Deep South has a culture and a value system all its own. I was taught to give respect to your parents and elders, treat others as you would want to be treated, and to trust your inner instincts. It's these little lessons that I have used to help me find my way through this life and I feel fortunate that I grew up in such a great state, in a time that was filled with challenges that forced me to look for answers. I have found that as I grow older, I long for the things I enjoyed as a kid in Mississippi—floating Black Creek, running trot lines for catfish, fishing for bream and bass, deer hunting and duck hunting, driving down old muddy roads and four-wheeling into deer camp—so many things that I cannot possibly list them all. It's these Mississippi-based memories that I now cherish.

As I look forward to my transition from being a lifelong working stiff to being a retired person within the next ten years, I see Mississippi in my future! It's a bright and sunny road that lies ahead of me and I intend to follow it right back to where I came from: Mississippi. I have heard that you can take the boy out of Mississippi, but you can't take Mississippi out of the boy! I can honestly say that where I am concerned, this is a true statement! I know this because I live every day with Mississippi in my blood, and I'm proud of it.

Marco St. John

Marco St. John has been a professional actor all his adult life, working in New York, Los Angeles, Europe, and most recently in Louisiana's budding film industry. He has appeared on Broadway, off-Broadway, and in regional theater, and has a solid background in Shakespeare, having played Hamlet when he was twenty-eight years old. He has had leads in soap operas (*As the World Turns*) and other network television programs and has appeared in around fifty films.

My mother was a Mississippi girl born and bred in the small coastal town of Ocean Springs. My dad came to New Orleans from Guatemala. They met over in Ocean Springs and moved to New Orleans shortly after they married. When they divorced some fourteen years later, Mom came back to Ocean Springs while my dad went to New York City. The coast was always the home place for me growing up. Then I went to college in New York to be with my father. My senior year I decided to be an actor after seeing a Broadway play, *The Five Finger Exercise*, with Brian Bedford. I felt I could do that and it was something I wanted to do. After graduation and a short stint in the army, I set about pursuing a career. After only two years of "struggling," working as a furniture mover while going to scene study classes and auditions, I met my wife and got married. I started to get jobs—first summer stock, then off-Broadway, and after a couple of more years, Broadway.

I was extremely dedicated and lived quite a full life, working hard to support us and making a life, going to classes and getting jobs wherever

I could find them. The jobs came slowly at first. Two summers of summer stock, then getting plays here and there, one in a restaurant owned by the husband of my acting teacher, then several off-Broadway productions. Looking back, I see that they actually came in rapid succession, although at the time it felt like a snail's pace. Then came my first Broadway play, *Poor Bitos*, by Jean Anouilh, produced by Hal Prince. From then up until the time just shy of my thirtieth birthday, I had what anyone would term a robust and very successful career in New York theatre, television, and film. All told, I was in eleven Broadway productions, all but one of them leading roles. In the last play I did, *Forty Carats*, I played the male lead opposite Julie Harris and it was a huge hit. That same year, I also had one of the starring roles in a soap opera, *As the World Turns*.

I left the play and the soap opera and lost a six-picture movie deal about that time, so my wife and I decided to take our son and go to California to try the movies. We stayed there a year and I did some television, but then we decided to return "home" to New York. Things were picking up again; I did the play *Timon of Athens*, for the New York Shakespeare Festival in Central Park, and during the run of that play something happened that would change my life forever.

I came off stage at the end of the first act and a stage manager came running up to me and said, "Your wife's been cut; you have to go; the police called. I'll get your understudy ready." I was stunned and rushed to my dressing room and changed. No one ever leaves a play midway through a performance, especially a lead.

I caught a taxi outside Central Park and after what seemed like an eternity got out in front of our five-floor walk-up in Greenwich Village on Perry Street. I ran upstairs and into our apartment; the door was wide open, all the lights were on, and there was not a single thing standing upright. It looked like a terrible fight had happened, or a wrecking crew had been there. I ran into the bedroom and there was a huge pool of blood on the floor of the antechamber. The bed had been put on its side and was leaning against a wall; on the floor was a chalk drawing of a body sprawled out.

I remember thinking it was like in the movies, but this was real.

I rushed out the front of the apartment to the stairway. When I got there, a policeman had his gun drawn and he stuck it in my face.

"I'm the husband," I said.

"Come with me," was all he replied.

Without saying a word, we drove a few blocks to St. Vincent's Hospital on Seventh Avenue. The lobby was filled with police. I just stood there dumbfounded until I heard a commotion and looked to see what it was; a policeman came over and stood in front of me to keep me away from a knot of people who came rushing out of a doorway. They were frantically, it seemed, pushing my wife on a gurney to an elevator and then into it. I guess they were worried I would make a lunge towards her and the gurney. A doctor came up to me. "They're taking her up to the operating room," he said. "We're doing everything we can, there are seven doctors working on her now." I fell down on my knees—seven doctors? She'll never make it, I thought. I felt people staring at me as though I was a bruised animal, and I guess I was. After a while a doctor with an angry look on his face came towards me. "She's gone," was all he said.

I felt some huge cord being cut, as a rope holding a ship to a pier and I suddenly was adrift with no anchor. I got up and walked out of the hospital. Our son—I had to find out what had happened and where he was. I walked numbly towards our home. I felt someone alongside of me. It was a police sergeant. He walked the rest of the way with me to our apartment building. His quiet strength steadied me. Our son was at a brownstone across the street, with a neighbor who had two young sons his same age.

My wife had seen me to the subway that night as I went to work. The police theorize that after she left me she went to the grocery store and from there someone followed her home. Our son was playing stick ball in the street in front of the building with the other children, so whoever it was must have seen her talk to him and knew that the door would be open. They followed her upstairs and confronted her in our apartment. She had yelled out the window for our son to stay outside and not come up. The police felt that the intruder had wanted her to get him upstairs so that he could kill him as well and there would be no witnesses. When she didn't do that, and told him instead to stay outside in the street, that must have triggered the fight between her and the intruder. She fought for her life, and gave her life for her son. There was no rape, only the brutal fight and then in the bedroom a gun wrapped in a pillow and a murder. Two twenty-dollar bills were gone from a change plate in my dressing area. No one was ever arrested for it. The police theorize it was a random act, but they could never be certain, and since I had a high profile as a successful Broadway actor, they would not discount that somehow had something to do with it. I had wanted to keep my son with me in New York, but the police convinced me, and my mother who had come up to help out, that this was not a good idea. After we buried my wife, Barbara, in her parents' plot in Point Pleasant, New Jersey, my mother left with my son to return to her husband in Ocean Springs. My father, who was also in New York, concurred; he knew I was almost insane with grief over our lives being ripped apart like this.

I stayed in New York for a while to close up our apartment and make plans for the future. I recognized later that I was fairly well off my rocker about the murder. I had heard the police say, in an off-the-cuff remark, that the killer could be hanging out in bars in the East Village. I took to drinking heavily and hanging out in bars there thinking to make a target of myself if there was indeed anyone looking for me. I ended up getting into several bad fights. A film offer came and it was to be shot in Europe; my dad, my mom, my agent, and my friends all felt it would be good for me to get out of the country and to work, so I went down to Mississippi, saw my son briefly, then took the job and left.

After I came back from Europe, I saw my son again, and then went to California, rented a house, and pursued a career there for a year. My mother brought my son out for a visit; then I went back to New York to live. I was finding it hard to stay in any one place, but my career started going again. I played a lead in a prime time television series and started getting more movie work. I had a lead in a film with Sean Connery. All the while I missed my son, who was in Mississippi with my mother. Then one day, sitting in my apartment, I realized that even with my series and films and continuing work there was still an empty hole where my heart was supposed to be. I asked myself, "What am I doing here?" and I couldn't come up with a good enough answer to suit me. I had a family in Ocean Springs, I reasoned, and I didn't want to be without them any longer. So I returned to Mississippi, and I've been here ever since.

I've kept acting, though it's not like it used to be, and I do other things, and there is a film industry in Louisiana now, so I work a fairly decent amount. I got married again to a spirited woman, Lorraine, and we have several houses. I also have a total of four children and stepchildren now and several grandchildren. I've returned to my Catholic faith and we go to church on Sundays. Living in Mississippi, after calling New York City home for twenty-five years, is a bit of a cultural jolt and I find myself a curious hybrid which is difficult for even me to comprehend. I have a lot of empathy for my wife and friends as they struggle to understand just where the hell I'm coming from most of the time, and I am blessed with a large circle of friends. Mississippi is nothing if not a breeding ground of friendships.

Since returning and living here for quite a while now, I have developed more of a Mississippi identity than I had as a young man, but it is grafted to a distinct New York experience, sensibility, and personality. Consequently, it always amuses me to hear the stereotypes the rest of the country sometimes has of Mississippians—especially now that I am one. If they only knew, I think to myself, chuckling at the view from both sides, and a response that was suggested to me comes to mind and seems appropriate: we bleed, we hurt, we honor family, we take comfort in our home and faith and struggle to overcome, like everyone else in the world.

J. Dale Thorn

J. Dale Thorn enjoyed a career in journalism, politics, and higher education in Louisiana before retiring to his native Mississippi. At Louisiana
State University he was a professor of mass communication, teaching
courses in writing, media law, public relations, and public opinion.
He also served as a university vice president and on the Louisiana
Board of Regents as associate commissioner of higher education. A
former marine, he holds bachelor's and master's degrees from LSU and
a doctorate from Florida State University. He is a native of McComb and
currently lives in Brandon.

Life's mystique takes us down transformative trails, with memories
that leave us to wonder. In my teens, although I loved Louisiana, I
learned to be thankful for my native Mississippi and the redemp-
tion it offered an ancestor. My great-grandfather Jesse's relocation to
Mississippi was the stuff of legend. His nineteenth-century ride from
Smith County, Texas, to Smith County, Mississippi, constituted a
criminal act on which my destiny would pivot.

The first time I heard that Grandpa Jesse had escaped Texas while
on trial for murder, I shuddered. It was only in middle age that I learned
the victim of Jesse's gunshot had survived. It was just attempted murder, I rationalized.

Nonetheless, as I learned from reading the trial record, Jesse, rather
than face Texas justice, chose to leap through a courthouse window
onto a waiting horse and ride to Mississippi, the land of his redemp-
tion. He died in 1941, an honored deacon in his church. I always wished

I could have heard of his wild ride from his own lips, but he died before I was born.

We, his descendants, would like to say that maybe Grandpa Jesse just had a case of wanderlust. We do know better. Yet his grandson, my father, must have had an early case of wanderlust. Either that or he was ready to be free of the farm. In either case he arrived in Louisiana in his teens, a student at Acadia Baptist Academy, a prep school of sorts for young men studying for the ministry. The school had been founded in 1917 in Eunice, the heart of Cajun, Catholic southwest Louisiana. Records indicate that after dormitories were erected a few years later, the school accepted its first class of boarders, eighty-six young men. The academy made it through the Depression and World War II but folded in 1973. My father, James, would recall his years there as among the most enjoyable of his life.

James apparently revered his grandpa Jesse as well, for I was named for Jesse. And no doubt my father fell for Louisiana. He married a Louisiana girl, and except for a couple of years in Texas, I spent my formative years in Louisiana. I, too, learned to love the place, developing a special regard for Louisiana girls, no doubt fostered in part by a wonderful mother and grandmother. From the age of six my folks sat my brother, Truett, and me down and had us listen to Louisiana election returns. Those were evenings a child never forgets, and soon I began to develop just a trace of an understanding of Louisiana's flamboyant politics. I could not know then that I would one day serve one of Louisiana's historic governors.

My brother had married a Mississippi girl and earned a degree at Mississippi College. And, sooner than I could have imagined, Mississippi began to tug at me. The first time I noticed it, I think, was while leaving an LSU–Ole Miss football game in Jackson. At first I dismissed the tug. Don't be foolish, I thought, you couldn't feel anything like that. But over the years the pull became more apparent.

My Mississippi relatives were and are a wonderful bunch. As I neared eligibility for early retirement, my dear cousin Dot Upton, a recent widow, began to hint that I should feel welcome to share her home in Rankin County if I decided to return to Mississippi. Just to share her cooking would be extraordinary, I thought. Dot was a grand-daughter of my great-grandfather Jesse. She could remember him.

One day I had the pleasure of having lunch over in the Smith County home of Meliter Pennington, the mother of Rankin County Sheriff Ronnie Pennington. I knew we were somehow related, but imagine my surprise when I learned that not only did the sheriff and I share the same great-grandfather—Jesse—but Meliter was also related to my grandmother Clara's side of the family, the Keenes.

The tugs continued, despite my thinking that this couldn't be happening. Having lived in Mississippi for less than a year after being born in McComb, I found the attraction to my native state surprising. Just to think of "coming home" to Mississippi added a new dimension to life. Despite her flaws and her stormy history, Mississippi beckoned.

Still, Louisiana had been my land of opportunity. Shortly after coming home from the Marine Corps I had two job offers from Monroe newspapers, and that was before I completed my first semester of college. Besides newspaper work, I was playing weekends in a rock 'n' roll band.

Later, I would become a state capitol correspondent and, while attending LSU, where I had a double major in history and journalism, would begin to grow intellectually, at least to the extent of exploring nuance and context. Learning that Colonel William Tecumseh Sherman had been the first president of LSU and happened to love the South belied much of the myth surrounding that despised Yankee warrior.

To grow intellectually one had to develop skepticism for matters widely regarded as certainties. LSU's Professor T. Harry Williams, an authority on the Civil War and Reconstruction, once told his students, of whom I was one, that as late as the 1960s at LSU it was difficult to teach the Civil War, for his students arrived with romantic ideas about the Lost Cause.

He might have added that Mississippi and Louisiana felt the sword of that war and its aftermath like no other states. The largest postwar expense in Mississippi's budget provided artificial limbs for Confederate veterans. Before the war, the wealthiest section of the United States was the stretch from Natchez to New Orleans. After the war, with cotton crops decimated and slaves emancipated, the two states lay impoverished. From Bilbo to Barnett, Mississippi governors played the race card. Louisiana governors didn't do much better. In both states, a hundred years after the Civil War, black citizens were denied the right to vote.

It was during my time as a capitol correspondent and interim editorial page editor at the *Times* of Shreveport that I received the least expected job offer of my career. A young Cajun congressman, Edwin Edwards, planned to run for governor in 1971. A year before the first primary he approached me about running his Washington office while he spent most of his time in Louisiana. It was easy to develop a high regard for the young Edwards. As a state senator he had come within one vote of eliminating Louisiana's boondoggle Sovereignty Commission. He was one of the few southerners to support the Voting Rights Act of 1965, and he did it his first year in Congress, a time when he might well have encountered a race-baiting opponent. Lyndon Johnson summoned Edwards to the White House to tell him he was impressed. Like many of us who had watched Edwin, the president regarded the new congressman as brilliant and courageous. I was honored to join Edwards's Washington staff.

When he won the governor's race, I returned to Baton Rouge to serve as his press secretary. Edwards's shortcomings have been so well documented and, alas, punctuated by a prison term, that I will belabor those on another occasion. For now it's enough to say that I found it more fun to work for Edwin when I was in Washington and he was in Louisiana than when we were both in Baton Rouge. Still, he had given me the opportunity to see Washington and its politics up close, and I tried to remember that with gratitude.

Eager to leave the governor's office, I took an opportunity to work at the state board of regents and began to watch Edwards from a distance. Even though I had observed him up close, I had never found his humor more biting. Of his 1983 opponent, who at times seemed indecisive, Edwards said it took an hour and a half for Dave Treen to watch *Sixty Minutes*. Edwards won the election with ease and went on to be indicted twice for corruption, the first trial ending in a hung jury, the second ending with a verdict of not guilty. It was enough to cause Edwin to drop out of the 1987 governor's race.

By 1991, I was teaching at LSU when Edwin and David Duke, the Nazi-like Klansman who would later serve a prison term as well, clashed in what most observers viewed as "the governor's race from hell." The incumbent governor, Buddy Roemer, a reformer, ran third. Roemer had made his share of mistakes, a list too long for this space, and Louisiana had a history of throwing reformers overboard after one term.

The bumper stickers in the Edwards-Duke race were all but unspeakable. "Vote for the Crook. It's Important," one said. My students were overheard saying, "This is embarrassing." Occasionally they would tell me they couldn't wait to leave Louisiana. I felt for them. Edwards swamped Duke for a fourth-term victory despite failing to win a majority of white votes. The one thing the two candidates had in common, Edwards observed, was that they were "both wizards under the sheets."

I confess, the stark choice in Louisiana made Mississippi look like a haven. At age fifty-eight I made the move. I found Mississippi inviting. Haley Barbour, once the political director in the Reagan White House, took the governor's office within a couple of years. He proved astute in dealing with Hurricane Katrina in 2005; his Louisiana counterpart seemed to struggle. In her defense it should be noted that if the levees had held, New Orleans would not have flooded.

In 2011, as the Mississippi River was threatening to flood both states, an unrelated anniversary brought Mississippi to the fore in a way that resonated around the country. To celebrate the fiftieth anniversary of the Freedom Rides, Barbour invited the riders to breakfast at the Governor's Mansion. It was a far cry from their earlier reception in Mississippi, when they were marched off to Parchman penitentiary to serve forty-day sentences.

For years I had tried to block from my mind a young black marine acquaintance. Casual friends, we decided at Christmastime 1960 to take a bus to Louisiana together, him to his home in New Orleans, me to my home in Monroe. The excitement of leaving boot camp behind in California was palpable.

At Big Spring, Texas, the bus stopped for lunch, and we received the abrupt notice that the lunch counter served whites only. People of color would have to eat elsewhere; just where I wasn't sure. I wish I could say I wasn't absolutely speechless; I was. I was eighteen and recall only my mind and heart wrestling with the burden of injustice.

Lunch added to the burden, and I had a hard time facing my fellow marine thereafter. It did not help that from there on he, wearing the same uniform and rank as I, was required to sit at the back of the bus. In Louisiana I bid him farewell. The next I heard of him he was dead, having committed suicide.

"We apologize to you for your mistreatment in 1961," Barbour told his breakfast audience half a century later, "and we appreciate this chance for atonement and reconciliation." He saluted them for "your courage, your commitment, your sufferings and your sacrifices."

I thought of others who had suffered the indignity of the back of the bus and whites-only lunch counters, of the countless veterans who volunteered to serve their country in war and peace, only to find that their country showed no respect for their constitutional rights back home.

Barbour's words, coupled with my own experience, were a reminder that the modern civil rights legislation freed whites as well from giving silent witness to irrational injustice.

The Freedom Riders gave the governor a standing ovation.

Jo McDivitt

Jo McDivitt was born in Pontotoc and grew up in Amory, in north Mississippi. She is a writer and newspaper publisher and formerly a flight at-
tendant with United Airlines, a publicist at Niki Singer, Inc., in New York
City, and host of a Memphis talk radio show, *A Cup of Jo*. She was a recipient of a 2011 Spirit of Women Spirit in Action award. She now lives
in the piney woods of Hattiesburg with her five adopted shelter pets.

I returned to the gardens of my childhood after leaving footprints all
over the world for over thirty-seven years.

I lived in New York City while roaming Marrakech, Paris, Rome,
Bangkok, Florence, Lisbon, and other ports, looking hither and yon for
the brass ring, a silver platter, a perfect sunset, and the indescribable
balm that gives a free spirit a sense of place. A sense of place is not to
be confused with a sense of belonging. I never needed to belong, to be
a part of the "in" crowd, a status seeker, or to reside in the brief, flicker-
ing light of fame. I yearned to find my sense of place—a place to greet
me with a smile each morning and a lullaby before slumber each night.

Thomas Wolfe wrote the famous, still widely read book *You Can't
Go Home Again*, published posthumously in 1940. I set out six and a
half years ago to prove his bittersweet theory wrong by hopefully, tri-
umphantly returning to Mississippi.

I returned to the gardens of my childhood carrying a cargo of books,
over three hundred hats (a harmless, happy trademark), and various
baubles and antiquities that do not guarantee one iota of satisfaction

beyond an appreciative glimpse to admire their originality and one-of-a-kind beauty.

My landing pad is a spot in the woods of south Mississippi on five acres in an old-fashioned, forgotten neighborhood. I located close enough to my beloved mama in north Mississippi to stay in touch while keeping a slice of freedom.

A renovated guest house near my main home did not lure Mama into abandoning the tiny white cottage where she elected to see the world through rose-colored glasses, creating her own semi-idyllic sense of place in this big world. She carefully and quietly buried all disappointments in a postage-stamp-sized garden, allowing the earth to absorb her tears.

Mama was happy to see my winged feet anchored back on the red clay soil of Mississippi. As always, she encouraged me to follow my passions and soar like a hawk, sometimes diving down from the clouds to prey upon some essential need. Before relocating to the heavens, she said, "Jo, I wish we had the money to make your little newspaper successful." I gently explained that the money was unnecessary. I was simply glad she liked the Mississippi grassroots newspaper that I started on a shoestring budget and a prayer when I came home.

As the calendar pages flew by, with Mama's eighties ticking ominously toward ninety, I knew it was a part of my destiny to reunite with this unselfish parent, as death, an unbidden and unwelcome shadow, periodically knocked at her door. I was back with the one friend and parent who loved me whether my decisions were wise or unwise. Her dinosaurian style of parenting built a foundation of self-confidence that cannot be attained by following wanderlust around the world. This priceless gift is indelibly stitched in my soul.

I did not readily fit into my chosen environs of south Mississippi, finding that the words of Thomas Wolfe, "you can't go home again," continued to play a game of tug-of-war throughout the days of inhabiting my nest in the woods. The title of Wolfe's novel comes from its finale, when protagonist George Webber realizes, "You can't go back home to your family, back home to your childhood . . . back home to a young man's dreams of glory and of fame . . . back home to places in the country, back home to the old forms and systems of things which once seemed everlasting but which are changing all the time—back home to the escapes of Time and Memory." His words boldly infiltrate the ranks of brave souls who once upon a time decided to pack their bags to seek fame, fortune, and love far away from home.

In the self-imposed south Mississippi lonely place that I named Walden Pond South, I was forced to be on my own in the middle of the woods. In Mississippi, newcomers and returning native sons and daughters are often greeted in wonderment, as in, "Why are you here?" Why, indeed! Have they forgotten that a big bowl of fresh black-eyed peas and black skillet cornbread are better than caviar, vintage champagne, and other palatable temptations? Fried green tomatoes win over escargot! And, if you are fortunate enough to have a fresh slice of a three-layer caramel-iced cake, you will forget the finest crème brûlée.

I have gotten to know myself better than ever during this recent stay in Mississippi. I've read my way through splendid books (waiting for every American citizen at no charge on the library shelves). Reading is another of Mama's enduring legacies passed on to me.

I'm happily reacquainted with favored fictional friends from the past including *Cheri*, from the French author of the perfect word, Colette; Hemingway's semiautobiographical ambulance driver in *A Farewell to Arms*; Pat Conroy's stable of realistic southern characters from *The Great Santini*, featuring the unforgettably cruel father figure, "Bull" Meecham; and Eudora Welty's much-read pages of great stories, including *The Optimist's Daughter*, describing southerners to the world unlike any other Mississippi author. A stack of books rivaling the Leaning Tower of Pisa is waiting by my bed. I first heard the term "bedside reading" in north Mississippi when I was a mere tadpole.

I am now preparing for another chapter of my peripatetic life, as Henry David Thoreau did after his stay at Walden Pond. He spent two years at Walden Pond writing his book *Walden*. I have been home again at Walden Pond South for six and a half years. I have penned two books that I have not sought to publish. I identify my time spent in these southern woods with Thoreau's at Walden Pond, even his memorable quote about living there. Thoreau said, "I went to the woods because I wished to live deliberately, to front only the essential facts of life, and see if I could not learn what it had to teach, and not, when I came to die, discover that I have not lived."

Will I dust off my elegant hobo sack of belongings, finally admitting Mr. Wolfe's time-worn treatise *You Can't Go Home Again* is true? I do not know. There are still whispers of beautiful words recalling me to Mississippi:

> The world caught me and harnessed me.
> And drove me through the dust, thirty years away from home.
> Migratory birds return to the same tree.
> Fish find their way back to the pools where they were hatched.
> I have been over the whole country,
> And have come back at last to the gardens of my childhood.
> My farm is only ten acres.
> The farm house has eight or nine rooms.
> Elms and willows shade the back garden.
> Peach trees stand by the front door.
> The village is out of sight.
> You can hear the dogs bark in the alleys,
> And cocks crow in the mulberry trees.
> When you come through the gate into the court
> You will find no dust or mess.
> Peace and quiet live in every room.
> I am content to stay here the rest of my life.
> At last I have found myself.

> Excerpt from the poem "I Return to the Place I Was Born"
> T'ao Yüan-ming (T'ao Qian), Chinese, 365–427

Sam Haskell

Sam Haskell, a native Mississippian, rose through the ranks of the famed William Morris Agency to become one of the most powerful agents in the television industry. As Worldwide Head of Television for the agency, he represented many Hollywood luminaries. He also packaged such megahit television shows as *The Cosby Show*, *Everybody Loves Raymond*, *Live with Regis and Kathie Lee*, and *Who Wants to Be a Millionaire*. He was named by *Television Week Magazine* as "One of the 25 Most Innovative and Influential People in Television for the Last 25 Years." He is the author of a best-selling memoir, *Promises I Made My Mother*. He and his wife, former Miss Mississippi Mary Donnelly, have two children and reside in Oxford, Mississippi.

W hen Judy Garland's character, Dorothy Gale, exclaimed, "There's no place like home!" in the classic MGM feature film *The Wizard of Oz*, it made adults and children alike think of home and count their blessings from coast to coast, and eventually throughout the entire world. The year was 1939, and in a year some claim to be the finest year in motion picture history (*Gone With the Wind*, *Stagecoach*, *Goodbye, Mr. Chips*, *The Women*, and *Mr. Smith Goes to Washington* were also released in 1939), *The Wizard of Oz* distinguished itself as one of the most endearing and enduring films of all time. I saw the film for the first time as a small boy, growing up in Amory, Mississippi. CBS had bought the rights to televise the film annually, and Judy Garland, starring in her own television series on CBS in the midsixties, hosted that first broadcast of *The Wizard of Oz* with actor Ray

Bolger, who costarred with Judy as the Scarecrow in the film. After the telecast, I told my mother that I was grateful to have such a wonderful home in Mississippi, and that no matter where I might end up as an adult, Mississippi would always be my home. Though only ten years old at the time, and determined to one day move to Hollywood, I somehow knew in my heart that there was truly no place like my Mississippi home.

After graduating from Ole Miss in 1977, and spending an additional year at the university working on a master's degree in communications, I was able to spend extra time in Oxford while my girlfriend, Mary Donnelly (now my wife of thirty years), reigned as Miss Mississippi 1977. In August of 1978, after Mary had crowned a new Miss Mississippi, I packed my car like a suitcase and drove directly to Los Angeles to pursue my dreams. Though I would miss everyone and everything I was leaving in Mississippi, I knew that I would return often, and eventually move back home permanently when my adventures were completed. But the adventures I had dreamed of could only be realized in California, not in Mississippi.

As I have discussed previously in my memoir, *Promises I Made My Mother*, after arriving in Los Angeles, I was hired to work in the mail room of the prestigious William Morris Agency, then was plucked from the mail room by the head of the TV department within five months and promoted to a full agent thirteen months later. I was soaking up everything as quickly as I could, and learning each and every thing necessary to become successful as a William Morris agent. I eventually became Worldwide Head of Television for the agency. The lessons of honesty, character, understanding, integrity, and class that had been instilled in me by my Mississippi mother, Mary Kirkpatrick Haskell—lessons simple in their explanation, but profound in their execution—helped pave the way for me to represent actors like Bill Cosby, Dolly Parton, Kathie Lee Gifford, Whoopi Goldberg, Ray Romano, Brook Shields, Sela Ward, George Clooney, Marilu Henner, Kirstie Alley, Tony Danza, Lucie Arnaz, Michael Feinstein, Liza Minnelli, Jean Smart, Delta Burke, Kathy Ireland, Lily Tomlin, Ann-Margret, Martin Short, and His Royal Highness The Prince Edward.

I had also become friends with Oscar-winning actors like Bette Davis, Olivia De Havilland, Morgan Freeman, and Red Buttons. My childhood dreams growing up in Mississippi had come true. I had become a part of a world I had only read about in books: a world where dreams could become reality if you know how to work hard and nurture your relationships. And, as my relationships with these iconic Hollywood actors deepened, sooner or later they would each join me in Mississippi for fund-raisers and gala concerts in support of college scholarships through the Mary Kirkpatrick Haskell Scholarship Foundation and "Stars Over Mississippi" (founded in memory of my mother), Hurricane Katrina relief through "Mississippi Rising," and the founding of the Trent Lott Leadership Institute at Ole Miss through "A Celebration of Leadership" at the Kennedy Center in Washington, DC, to name a few. Each of these important charities was aided by my friends who had all decided to "come home" with me to help.

Throughout my thirty years in Hollywood, all of my special friends and clients were always willing to help me help my beloved Mississippi. My mother, whom I lost to cancer twenty-five years ago, taught me as a child the importance of sharing your blessings with those in need. I have always tried to provide infrastructures for people to step up to do something good to benefit others. Basically, I believe everyone wants to do something good, and when you show them the way, they *will* step up to the plate. The philanthropic part of my life has been built on this premise, and my special friends have "come home" with me many times to help.

After thirty years in Hollywood, and after packaging such hit shows as *The Cosby Show*, *Everybody Loves Raymond*, *Fresh Prince of Bel Air*, *Diagnosis Murder*, *Live with Regis and Kathie Lee*, *Who Wants to Be A Millionaire*, *Sisters*, *Las Vegas*, and *Lost*, I knew it was finally time to go home. Mary and I missed our friends and families, and their love, which was all waiting for us back home. We wanted to wrap ourselves in a metaphorical blanket known as Mississippi and let it comfort us and protect us. Mary and I had raised our children Sam IV and Mary Lane in Los Angeles, and they were both in college and planning their own futures, so we announced to the world that we were ready to pack up and head home to Mississippi.

We had purchased land in Oxford a dozen years earlier, with plans of building our dream home there. Construction began in late 2007, and by January 2010, we were ready to make the move to our new home, Magnolia Hill, in Oxford. I was producing the 2010 Miss America Pageant in Las Vegas when the trucks pulled into the driveway of our Monterey Colonial Home in Encino, California. Mary likes to joke that "while she was packing and moving, Sam was hanging out with fifty-three of the most beautiful women in America." She may have been right, but truly the most beautiful woman I know was preparing for our "journey home." Mary is the heart and soul of my life and our family. I finished producing the pageant, and then went back on the road to complete the second leg of my national book tour for *Promises I Made My Mother*. I finally arrived home in late February, and Mary, her sister, Leslie Wilson, our housekeeper, Anna, and a few wonderful friends had each worked hard to unpack, organize, and start making Oxford our new home.

It was the easiest transition I could have ever imagined, mainly because Mary was determined that it not be stressful for *me*—and that's why I love her so much. Yes, she's beautiful, talented, and wise, but she always puts me and the children first, and she knew I would be a wreck about this move home. We loved our thirty years in California, but we also knew it was time to leave. But leaving meant packing thirty years of our lives into three eighteen-wheeler trucks. I had arrived in 1978 in a car with everything I owned packed in every nook and cranny inside it, and when we returned to Mississippi three decades later, it took three gigantic freight trucks to carry the four tons of furnishings, china, crystal, books, photographs, and collectibles that made our lives complete.

Magnolia Hill houses everything now, and being home with those we love most in this world has exceeded our expectations. So many of our close college friends regularly visit or have retired to our beloved Oxford, Mississippi. We have loved every minute of our time here, and have cherished every old and new friend who crosses our path, because you see, in the words of Dorothy Gale, "There's no place like home."

(Written on August 6, 2011, the thirty-third anniversary of my arrival in Los Angeles after leaving Mississippi)

Johnnie Mae Maberry

Johnnie Mae Maberry is a Jackson native who graduated from Tougaloo College with a bachelor's degree in art/art education and Mississippi College with a master's degree in art education and an MFA. A prolific artist, Maberry produces 3-D paintings, drawings, prints, sculptures, and mixed media compositions. She is an associate professor of art at Tougaloo College and the director of the Tougaloo Art Colony. Some of her most recent accomplishments include being a part of HBCU and other group exhibits featured in New York, Texas, Alabama, Georgia, South Carolina, Tennessee, Mississippi, and Maryland. Maberry's works can be viewed in the image gallery of http://www.slaveryinamerica.org, an educational website dedicated to offering a history of slavery in America, and also at http://www.ArtWanted.com.

Deddy's (we never said *daddy*) favorite saying was, "We will cross that bridge when we come to it." My deddy, Major Maberry, crossed the bridge into restful sleep at the youthful age of fifty-seven. During Deddy's short illness, I was living in Joliet, Illinois, which had been my home away from my Mississippi home for nearly twelve years. The year was 1983 and twelve years prior, I would never have dreamed of "crossing *that* bridge" into Illinois or any other state other than Mississippi.

Born in 1948, I grew up on Enochs Street in the Georgetown community of Hinds County. Living in this area of town with my parents, three sisters, and one brother set us apart by *black standards* as middle class. East of Georgetown was Virdition. I was fifty years old when I happened to notice a sign posted in the area that we called "Virdition" that read "Welcome to Virden Addition." I never questioned the pronunciation. Mama and Deddy always said "Virdition" and that is what it was. I grew up under Mama and Deddy's watchful and protective guidance. Mama was a housewife and Deddy was a roofing contractor who shared ownership in Maberry's Brothers Roofing with his younger brother, Walter.

Mama took care of us during the week and Deddy worked all day. When we children saw Deddy's truck pull into the driveway, we would jump up and down, singing, "Deddy's home, Deddy's home!" This we did daily and were rewarded with hugs, kisses, and dinner. When we were small children, we never ate dinner before Deddy came home from work. Sometimes his hands would be bandaged because of the burns that he sustained from the hot tar used on the rooftops.

It seems that I cannot recall a single instance during my childhood of wanting to leave home. Home to me was wherever Mama and Deddy lived. I recall the Christmas when Deddy sat all five of us down and explained that there would be no toys. He said that *colored* people would not be shopping in any of the stores in a united boycott. I also remember that on that particular Christmas I awakened to smells of fresh fruit, cakes, turkey dressing, and pineapple-glazed ham. Most spectacular was the image outside our big picture window. Clear ice covered the trees and bushes and the ground was also covered and dusted with a very thin layer of snow. I remember the Christmas of the boycott as being the most beautiful Christmas of my childhood; no commercial decorations could ever match the sparkle of light that gleamed from the ice-covered branches as they reflected the sunlight.

There are many memories that occasionally surface. I dreamed of becoming an artist. Deddy made me an easel out of scrap wood during a time when no one thought a black girl should have dreams of becoming an artist. Although a dreamer, I was not out of tune with reality. I was perhaps one of the first to rush out of the doors at Lanier High School in a 1960s protest against civil injustices, an event that nearly gave our principal, Mr. Buckley, a heart attack and that had parents rushing to pick up their "gone plum insane" teens and cart us home before the city police hauled us all off to jail. I realized early that *causes* gave me an adrenalin rush, and still do. While my sisters all said that they could not wait to leave this backwards place, I always said that I would remain in Mississippi to fight for causes.

Tougaloo College seemed to be a natural fit for me. It had to be, since I only applied to one college. One would think that after meeting and interacting with so many interesting students from different parts of the United States that I would begin to make plans to relocate. I did, indeed, make plans but they did not include relocating. Since all of my sisters had beaten me to the altar (including my younger sister), I announced my junior year of college that "I will marry whomever I am dating at the time (lucky guy) a month after I graduate from college." I made other announcements as well, but that singular one is the one that factors into my departure from Mississippi. On June 6, 1970, I married Johnny Gilbert, a month after my college graduation.

Unlike myself, my now ex-husband after thirty-seven years of marriage talked constantly about leaving Mississippi. I figured that after a few months of being "blissfully" happy with me, he would forget about moving. Three months after our marriage, he left as I packed up our small apartment, put things in storage, and made arrangements to follow him to Chicago, Illinois . . . or experience a very short marriage. Once again, I found myself crossing a bridge to fight for another cause.

The one thing that I discovered when I moved from Mississippi to Chicago is that I hated cold weather, black soil, and crowded streets. I adjusted to the situations of my new location. My first teaching experience was at an inner city school with broken windows and graffiti-scarred walls. I stood eye to eye with most of my students; added to that, my miniskirts and go-go boots did not make me a favorite of the female students. Becoming pregnant in December was my saving grace. I chose not to go back to that particular school in the spring.

Three years later we moved to Joliet, Illinois. We bought a house on the east side of town. It was an area that was once described as the "silk stocking" area of Joliet. Our house was once the house of the first mayor of Joliet. We fell in love with the French fireplace and winding staircase. Naively, we had bought a true money pit. The first time we decided to light the fireplace, smoke billowed from the frame of the fireplace. We debated if we should just let the place burn down.

Nine years later (we had three children and I was two months pregnant), Joliet was gradually becoming an unhappy place financially for us and educationally for our children. Then I received a call that my deddy had been diagnosed with cancer. I made numerous trips home during his illness. I cried the entire trip back to Joliet after visiting him for the last time. I knew then that the time had come to cross the bridge back to Mississippi.

Keith Thibodeaux

Keith Thibodeaux came to the world's attention as the drum-playing child prodigy in the role of Little Ricky in the classic comedy *I Love Lucy*. He went on to play in many more productions, including *The Andy Griffith Show*, appearing as Opie's best friend. While attending the University of Louisiana in Lafayette, Keith joined, recorded with, and toured with the rock band David and the Giants. In 1991, he joined his wife, Kathy, a silver medalist at the second USA International Ballet Competition (1982), on tour with her company Ballet Magnificat! He became executive director of the internationally recognized professional ballet company and ministry Ballet Magnificat!, which is headquartered in Jackson. He is the author of a memoir, *Life After Lucy*, which tells his life story after he left Hollywood and became a Christian. He and Kathy have one daughter, Tara, who is also a dancer and choreographer.

My earliest memories involve listening to music and keeping time by beating on pots and pans with sticks, knives, and forks. I liked to strike up a beat on the garbage cans outside the kitchen door of our house in Lafayette, Louisiana. With the sounds of Benny Goodman, Count Basie, and Duke Ellington filling our house, I quickly developed a sense of rhythm.

I got my first real drum when I was only two years old—a snare drum, a gift from my dad's friend, the local music teacher in Bunkie, the small town where my family had relocated. My dad talked up his kid with his unusual talent, and soon I was playing for the Lions Club and local talent shows. By three, I had been invited to attend the National Drummers Convention in Jackson, Mississippi. The newspapers were reporting on "Bunkie's infant prodigy, Keith Thibodeaux."

Amid the local hoopla about me, my dad heard about the *Horace Heidt Show*, a CBS-TV program featuring undiscovered professional talent. Somehow my uncle Terrell, who had always been very supportive of me and my drumming, managed to arrange an audition for me with Heidt's people, and they decided to put me on the show. When the big night came, I, a little bitty three-year-old, performed with Horace Heidt's orchestra to wild cheering and applause from the hometown crowd.

About two weeks later, Mr. Heidt called Dad and offered him three hundred dollars a week to tour with his show. My stunned father hesitated, and Mr. Heidt said, "Oh, all right, I'll make it five hundred for both of you, and that's it." At age three, just out of diapers, I had risen from drumming on trash can tops to touring with a big-name professional orchestra.

My tour with Mr. Heidt ended in 1955 on the West Coast. The taste of the big time was in Dad's blood now, and he thought there was more opportunity in California, so he moved the whole family west. Little did I realize that my life as a performer was just beginning.

Mom, a true southerner, didn't like California at first and said, "I feel as if we're living in a motel. It just doesn't feel homey to me." That was understandable, but Dad was head of the house and she didn't question him.

One day soon afterward, Dad heard through a friend that Lucille Ball and Desi Arnaz were conducting a talent search to find a little boy to play their TV son on *I Love Lucy*. Through his friend, Dad arranged my audition for the comedy series. We were in the car as Dad slowed down, nearing the gates of the Motion Pictures Center. "This is it, Keith," he smiled and said.

Inside the studio, while Desi and I took turns on the drums, I heard Lucy say excitedly, "This is the kid! This is him! This is Little Ricky!" I was five years old.

The first thing they did was give me a stage name, Richard Keith, because, Desi said, the name Thibodeaux was too hard and too long to remember, and people couldn't pronounce it.

I worked on *I Love Lucy* until the show closed in 1960, and began to occasionally appear with their son, Desi Jr., on the new *The Lucy Show*, which ran until 1965.

In 1962, I auditioned and won the role of Opie's best friend, Johnny Paul Jason, on the weekly *The Andy Griffith Show*. *Andy Griffith* was a great show—from the stories to the actual working relationships on the set. The laid-back and easy-going atmosphere was entirely different from the tense moments I'd experienced working on *I Love Lucy* with the perfectionist Lucille Ball and the mercurial Desi Arnaz. It wasn't unusual for the cast and crew of *The Andy Griffith Show* to sit around playing checkers during breaks. Both *The Andy Griffith Show* and *I Love Lucy* would go on to become classics and live forever in reruns.

I have read where child star Dean Stockwell said, "The life of a child star is so fraught with responsibilities that it frustrates normal interests and associations with other children. It's a miserable way to bring up a child." I was not miserable as a child, but I'd have to agree that acting does affect normal associations with other kids. At a time when most kids are carefree—their biggest worry is getting a good grade on a school quiz or making the Little League team—my life was becoming increasingly complicated. Not only did I have the normal school issues to deal with, but I also had to satisfy all the adults in my family and on the show.

Just as I was beginning to enjoy being a teenager, my family fell apart. My mother was moving back to Louisiana and my father was staying behind in California. I had often wondered about the Cajun country home I had left at the age of three, but I had few memories of it. As the plane took off and began to climb into the clouds above Los Angeles, my emotions were churning.

It was late one November evening at my mother's home in Lafayette when I received an unexpected call from David Huff of the rock band David and the Giants from Laurel, Mississippi. I knew the band quite well as they had played in town and I hung out with them occasionally. Recently, my band had a gig at a club in town and David came to watch me play, and now he was asking me to play the drums with his band. This band was popular throughout the South and I was going to be their drummer! It could not have come at a better time in my life. I had gotten heavily into the drug scene in Lafayette, and I desperately needed a change.

When I drove down a red dirt road to a shack in Laurel where the band practiced, hung out, and often slept, I realized that Laurel was light years away from Los Angeles. But I was glad to be there and I was glad to be sitting behind a set of drums again. We played all around the South, with many of our gigs at the Vapors Club in Biloxi, where Little Richard, Jimi Hendrix, the Allman Brothers (then called Allman Joy) played. Late nights turned into late sleeping with drugs and girls and alcohol, and my health began to suffer greatly.

I turned to God to ask for his help in straightening out my life. As a cradle Catholic, I had never established a spiritual relationship with God through the church. In 1974, I made my way back to Christianity and turned my life around. Those were special days for me in Laurel, but the guys in the band didn't understand this sudden change in me. On the long drives between college campuses in Oxford, Tuscaloosa, and Columbus, I began to witness to them.

On the luckiest day of my life, I met a ballet dancer while eating at a supper club on the reservoir in Jackson. Kathy Denton had probably put in more time at a ballet barre than I had behind the drums. She is a tall, thin, black-haired beauty, the perfect vision of a ballet dancer. We married after a three-month, whirlwind courtship. She went on to win a silver medal in the Second International Ballet Competition and then, with spirit and courage, formed her own ballet company, Ballet Magnificat!—a Christian company dedicated to sharing the good news of Jesus Christ through dance. While the school and management is located in Jackson, the company travels the world sharing its message in a unique way. I have put my drums on the shelf to help Kathy manage the dance company. Our daughter, Tara, is now training to follow her mother in her dance steps.

In our travels people are often astonished to find that this miracle of art and spirituality comes from Mississippi. Kathy and I are so proud that Ballet Magnificat! has become a wonderful ambassador for the Lord and for our state.

In a sense, I have been born three times: first, in Lafayette, Louisiana, the first child of Mary Ann and Lionel Thibodeaux; second, when Little Ricky was "born" on *I Love Lucy*; and finally, in 1974, when I first experienced the reality and truth of Jesus Christ. Maybe I ought to add a fourth birth—when I met Kathy Denton Thibodeaux. When our travels take us far away, and we finally come back to Jackson, Kathy and I heave a great sigh of contentment. Heaven is my real home, but Mississippi is the next best thing.

Maureen Ryan

Maureen Ryan is professor of English at the University of Southern Mississippi, where she served for many years as dean of the Honors College and currently teaches modern and contemporary American literature. Her publications include *The Other Side of Grief: The Home Front
and the Aftermath in American Narratives of the Vietnam War* (University of Massachusetts Press, 2008); *Innocence and Estrangement in the
Fiction of Jean Stafford* (Louisiana State University Press, 1987); and
essays on the work of Marilynne Robinson, Willa Cather, Bobbie Ann
Mason, Barbara Kingsolver, and Lillian Hellman, among others.

Lucinda Williams and Amos Lee toured together in the summer
of 2011. Gravelly voiced folk-rock-blues singer Lucinda Williams,
a true southern girl who has lived in Louisiana, Mississippi, and
Tennessee, has been kicking around a while, singing blues and betrayal
and bayous. But the very talented Amos Lee is a relative newcomer,
a Philadelphia native who graduated from the University of South
Carolina before returning home to teach elementary school, then on to
success as a singer-songwriter.

During a recent family visit back east, I joined cousins and graduate school friends at a Williams-Lee concert. After the concert, where
Lucinda Williams sang about "going back to the Crescent City/where
everything's still the same" and Amos Lee plaintively bid farewell to his
"southern girl," my bright, endearing, but decidedly parochial graduate school friend challenged me yet again about why I have lived, lo
these many years, in Mississippi—to him, the unlikeliest and most

unappealing of places. This incredulity from a man who will not leave Philadelphia for longer than a two-week vacation and who has not, in the almost thirty years that I've lived here, come to Mississippi to learn for himself why I love living here. He knows that I was lured to Mississippi many years ago, in a bad academic job market, for the tenure-track university position that seemed to me, despite its dubious location, preferable to the career of low-paying, tenuous, part-time teaching at community colleges in the Philadelphia area that so many of my emotionally place-bound graduate school colleagues reluctantly embraced. What he's never understood is why I stayed. And my old friend's skepticism about my affection for the South is largely my fault, because I find it oddly difficult to explain to him the ineffable satisfactions of living in Mississippi.

I mean, the obvious attractions of my life in the Deep South are easy to recount—a comfortable house that would cost three or four times as much in the mid-Atlantic area where I grew up (and to which my friend clings so intransigently). Weather that is enviably temperate seven or eight months of the year. Daily life in what is for Mississippi a sizeable city (Hattiesburg) that offers attractive small-city amenities: restaurants, a mall, a movie multiplex, a local bookstore—and Hudson's.

My doubting Yankee friend makes some good points, however, when he reminds me that that lovely late-fall-to-early-spring weather turns insufferably hot for a large lump of the year: June to August—May, September. Not to mention the lingering horrors of Hurricane Katrina's brief and devastating pass through my town. And, admittedly, the movie theatre never shows a foreign or independent movie, though I can see the superhero–special effects–action movie of the season starting every twenty minutes, on three or four different screens, in 2- or 3-D. And my nice house? Well, I didn't buy it until I'd lived in Hattiesburg for a dozen years, because I was sure that I would be moving away from Mississippi—any time now.

And then there's the race thing—the unspeakable, unspoken, untouchable taboo that looms over all matters southern. My never-coming-to-Mississippi old friend clings to all sorts of unsavory assumptions about racism in the South, though he lives in a large, messy city where racial relationships (which in Mississippi pretty much means black-white relationships) are every bit as vexed as they are in Chicago, Detroit, and New York. It's true that my earliest memories of relocating here are the local realtor who wouldn't show me an apartment in a secluded alley because "the 'boogers' might get you" and a retail shopkeeper who railed loudly to a store full of white customers about the black girl she'd caught shoplifting the day before. After almost thirty years in Mississippi, admittedly, I don't have many black friends. And I wish that the subtle warmth and unspoken solidarity that I felt from black townspeople, when they saw my Obama 2008 button during the last presidential campaign, had hung on a bit longer. But in daily living in Hattiesburg, my interactions with people of color are consistently civil, even courteous. And my many African American students are for the most part pleasant as well as eager to learn. I won't ingenuously suggest that racism has disappeared from Mississippi, but it's no more egregious than attitudes that my northeastern friend observes every day.

In fact, the uncommon civility of life in the South is—in an increasingly uncivil world—why I should have bought that house right away, why I have never left, why I have made Mississippi home. That's an intangible and seemingly minor characteristic of life in the South, which is why it seems an unacceptable explanation to my East Coast friend for why I like living here. Strangers acknowledge each other on the street or in a store. Drivers yield on the road when you're trying to merge or make a turn (ok, it's true that no one uses their turn signals, but still). This comfortable, easy quotidian surely cannot, for many people, compensate for more problematic aspects of small-city, southern life: the extreme political and social conservatism, the sometimes smug flaunting of "Christian" values, the lack of urban amenities. For many colleagues who have fled Mississippi for jobs in better universities, higher salaries, or more exciting cities, the enervating heat symbolizes an enervating life: narrow, closed, and dull. One of my graduate students, on her way home from summer study in England, noted on Facebook today that she "already feels the 'sipp depression setting in" (in response to which, a friend of hers commented, "Don't come back! Don't do it!"). I get that. It took me a couple of years to adjust to slow-moving, often myopic Mississippi as well. But all these years later, it's an easy, safe, and agreeable place to live. It's home.

Amos Lee must miss the South as well. In "Southern Girl," he sings that "something about a southern girl/make me feel right/in a Mississippi morning/she's an angel in flight." I think he captures my own inability to explain the South to my Philadelphia pal: I can't tell you *exactly* what, but there's "something about a southerner."

Mary Donnelly Haskell

Mary Donnelly Haskell, born in Beaumont, Texas, came to Ole Miss in the fall of 1976, where she met her future husband, Sam Haskell. She pledged Chi Omega sorority, represented Ole Miss in the Miss Mississippi Pageant, and won the crown. After completing her year as Miss Mississippi and graduating from Ole Miss in 1981, she moved to Los Angeles, married Sam the following year, and went on to have a successful television and recording career. She and her husband live in Oxford and are the parents of two children.

When people ask me where I'm from, I usually answer: "I was born and raised in Beaumont, Texas, but my mother's people are from Alabama, so I spent a great deal of time there growing up—but I'm *from* Mississippi."

In 1976, following in the steps of my older sister, Pride (who was at Ole Miss in the late sixties), I traveled to Oxford from my hometown of Beaumont, Texas, and entered the freshman class as a music major. Looking back, I see that so much of the path my future would take was defined by events that first year. First, I met my husband, Sam, just before classes started (in fact, he was my very first date at Ole Miss). I think the fact that I fell in love with and married a "Mississippi boy" could in itself qualify me as an adopted Mississippian. But there is another significant event that also played a big part in my deep connection to the people of this wonderful state.

At the beginning of the second semester, I was encouraged to enter the Miss University Pageant by my sorority, Chi Omega. I was fortunate enough to win that title and then represent Ole Miss in the Miss Mississippi Pageant that summer. At the age of eighteen, I was crowned Miss Mississippi and proudly headed to Atlantic City for the Miss America Pageant to represent my state! It was an amazing experience competing at Miss America, but even more wonderful was the opportunity I had to come back here and travel the state that year . . . in every town I visited, I experienced the hospitality and grace that is Mississippi. It think it would be impossible to travel this state as I did and not feel as though you are at the very least, an adopted Mississippian. My memories of that time and the pride I take in being a former Miss Mississippi are so very dear to me.

By the time I graduated from Ole Miss at the end of 1980, Sam had been in Los Angeles for several years and established his career with the William Morris Agency in Beverly Hills. I had the benefit of joining him in an already tight-knit circle of fellow Mississippians who were working in Hollywood at the time. What a difference that made in feeling part of a community—the "Mississippi Mafia" they called it—and that fellowship made for many an old fashioned potluck dinner or home-away-from-home Thanksgiving meal!

Sam and I had talked so often when we were dating at Ole Miss about following our dreams out to California, and there we were, surrounded by all the possibilities and challenges of lives and careers in the entertainment industry. We were blessed beyond words to live out those dreams for the almost thirty years we were in Los Angeles. We raised our children in the community of Encino, had a wonderful church family at Bel Air Presbyterian Church, and made many great friends, but at the same time we remained deeply connected to our Mississippi roots through the university, the Miss Mississippi Pageant, and most of all our family and friends. I've always said that we may have lived all those years in California, but in a lot of ways, we never left Mississippi!

When our children reached an age where we could seriously start thinking about where we wanted to spend our "golden years," there was no hesitation—it was always Mississippi—and more specifically, Oxford. We had always thought that it would be a dream come true to retire back where our life together began, at Ole Miss. And so the process began. Working with our dear friend Frank Tindall, we found the land and planned the house that we would build for our life back home in Oxford. We worked on the plans for our home over several years, on trips back to Oxford for ballgame weekends or special events, as well as during visits that Frank and his wife, Marsha, would make to our home in California. The building process lasted two years, and there were monthly trips to oversee the construction during 2009 and 2010. With each work trip I would make to Oxford, I became more and more anxious to be back home for good. Staying in the condo that had served as our weekend home for several years, I dreamed of the day we could be in our new home. So many choices we made about our new house had to do with making a home we could share with our family and friends.

I was being interviewed in California about moving back to Mississippi, and was asked the question, "What will you take with you to Mississippi?" I think the writer assumed I would say something about a piece of antique furniture or art, but my answer was very simple, and probably unexpected. I said, "Our friends." That is perhaps the single greatest joy about coming home to Mississippi—sharing it with others! Whether it's showing them Ole Miss, the square, or Rowan Oak in Oxford, driving down to Indianola or Greenwood to share our blues history, or just giving them their first taste of fried catfish out at Old Taylor, we *love* sharing all things Mississippi, especially its people!

We could not have dreamed of a more perfect experience than that of working with all the amazing people who shared in the building of our new home in Oxford—a designer's shared vision, a builder's commitment, and many craftsmen's gifted hands. How often does it happen that you dream about and plan something for years and then it turns out even better than you ever imagined? Our pastor back in California would say, "That's not odd; it's God." And I believe God did indeed shepherd us back to our home here in Mississippi. Our dream of coming home to Mississippi has been a dream come true. Coming home to a place of warmth and fellowship, a spirit of community and caring—we are so very blessed!

Bob Allan Dunaway

Bob Allan Dunaway is a retired art teacher and a native of Walthall County. He moved to Columbia, Mississippi, with his mother at the start of World War II. He became interested in photography and art, which he studied at Mississippi College after a tour in the air force. For thirty-five years he taught art in the Jackson public schools and at Mississippi College, Wayland Baptist College, and Hinds Community College. He maintains a studio in Clinton and continues to paint and pursue the joy of writing articles for the *Tylertown Times* entitled "Things Remembered." He is the author of *Things Remembered—Recollections about Recollections* and *DRAWING! . . . Where to Begin.*

When I was eleven years old, I became unhappy over something and decided I would leave home. I packed a small cardboard suitcase with a few clothes and comic books and hitchhiked about forty miles to my daddy's home. I felt sure he and my stepmother would take me in and solve all my problems. There I had no supervision and could do as I pleased. It was summer with no school days to worry about. But soon I missed my playmates and the routines established back at home, so I asked to be put on a bus and sent back. I was welcomed with open arms and a forgiving mother. Nothing had changed.

When I was all grown up, my travels outside Mississippi began with a tour in the U.S. Air Force which took me to Europe and North Africa for over two years. Letters from home always brought nostalgic memories of family and friends. I dreamed of getting back to familiar surroundings and events that had previously shaped my life. Little had changed among friends and relatives, except that my namesake grand-father had died, and most of my former classmates had graduated from college and were living elsewhere. Making new friends, however, was not difficult. Entering college myself, I encountered several former military members; we had much in common. Although I was depending on the GI Bill, the administrators told me I still must put a small portion down before I could be admitted. Those former GIs in line with me at registration pitched in enough dollars to allow me to start that semester. Those still living remain good friends to this day.

I became an art teacher and in a course of events sought advanced degrees which took me to Illinois and Arizona. Summers were spent in those places—meeting requirements needed for more pay and advancement. Most summers I had to leave family at home, so returning each time became a much-needed lift from the pressures of study. Friends were always there as well, and after a week or so, it was as if I had never left. Up until this time, it never occurred to me that work would take me totally away from Mississippi. With the exception of a sister in Arizona, all my family was nearby, down the road a piece, or across town. The opportunity arose for better pay and advancement, but it was in Texas, seven hundred and fifty plus miles away. Ambition, however, drove me to make the decision to move, so I bundled up a wife, three children, and a mother-in-law, and began a new life in the Texas panhandle.

After we grew accustomed to spending a lot of time in the cellar out of respect for many tornadoes and to a pool-table-flat landscape almost totally devoid of large trees, we began to become a part of the community and cultivate friends. Not often, but on occasion, Mississippi friends would pass through and stop for a brief visit. Relatives wrote and called with news about family and political goings-on, news that prompted thoughts of our being permanently apart from all those folks and our former lifestyle. I became aware that I really missed swimming and fishing in the Bogue Chitto River and would not be able to introduce my young children to the thrill of that experience. The nearest river to us at the time was hours away, and it really did not qualify as a river by Mississippi standards. The only thing familiar to someone from south Mississippi was the farming, although the method was a bit different, since it was necessary to irrigate crops due to lack of adequate rainfall.

I was determined to adjust, and as time went by, I felt the family was making progress in that direction. However, trips back to Mississippi to visit family always rekindled a desire to someday return. I imagined retirement, associations with old friends, walking familiar trails through familiar woods and fields, and painting pictures of those places that shaped my life in my youth. All this lingered in the back of my mind and tugged at the door of my heart every time I talked with friends and family back home. They would tell about current happenings there in such a way that made me feel I should still be a part of them, and my thoughts would linger on the conversation for days, even weeks.

As a youth, I had always been fascinated with flying. The best thing about Texas was that my new friends there had a passion for flying. They encouraged me to take lessons, and within the second year, I had earned my license and had developed a new respect for the Texas panhandle and its wide-open spaces. At five thousand feet, one could see Lubbock, Muleshoe, Floydada, and Canyon at the same time.

When my father died, I flew myself and my wife, Jeanette, back to Mississippi. We stopped first in Natchez, flying along the mighty Mississippi River the last half hour. My brother David met us there, and the three of us flew on to Tylertown by way of Enon, where we buzzed my aunt and uncle at the farm where I spent most of the summers while growing up. They waved as we made low passes over the garden where they were picking beans. My aunt later told me she knew it was me, remembering the time I told her someday I would fly and come see her.

Seeing the farm and surrounding countryside from above put it all in perspective for the first time. Many memories flooded my mind while I looked down at the pastures and farmland between Enon and Tylertown along the road we traveled in my granddaddy's old Model A truck.

In this curve was Alford's store, and in the fields beyond the store were Leatherwood Creek and my great-grandfather's home place. Approaching Tylertown I could see the house site where my memory first kicked in—I was three or four years old.

We spent a few days with family and friends and flew back to Texas. As time passed, I kept having visions of the Mississippi terrain from high above and could not avoid making comparisons to the Texas panhandle. That part of Texas has its intrinsic beauty, and the entire family enjoyed outings to learn more about it, but I kept the visions of my youth and the lifelong friendships in Mississippi constantly in my thoughts.

When the phone rang one day, and the dean at Hinds Junior College in Raymond asked me if I would be interested in coming back home to chair the art department, I almost immediately said yes. However, Jeanette had a job at Sears and we had all become active in our church, so I felt they should have some input in the decision. The two oldest children had started school and had made friends there and at church, so they were more at home in Plainview. We prayed about it and eventually became comfortable with the decision to return.

The Hinds dean that hired me turned out to be from the Texas panhandle. We established a wholesome professional relationship and worked together well for a year. We often talked about his early years growing up in Texas. Then one Monday I returned to work from a weekend of swimming in the Bogue Chitto with the children to find that the dean had resigned to return to Texas.

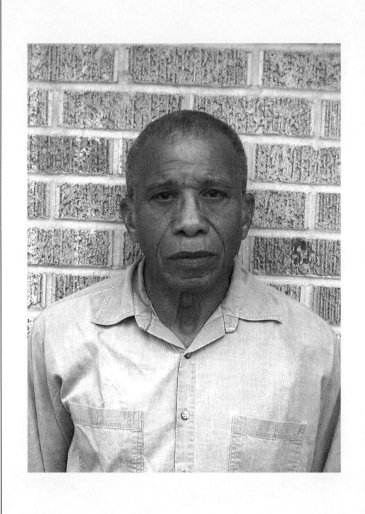

Jerry W. Ward, Jr.

Jerry W. Ward, Jr., is a Distinguished Scholar and professor of English at Dillard University and a Famous Overseas Professor at Central China Normal University (Wuhan). He spent thirty-two years as the Lawrence Durgin Professor of Literature at Tougaloo College. Recognized as one of the leading experts on Richard Wright, he is a founding member of the Richard Wright Circle and coeditor of *The Richard Wright Encyclopedia*. He received the Richard Wright Literary Excellence Award in 2011. His essays and poetry have been published in numerous literary journals. His recent books are *The Katrina Papers: A Journal of Trauma and Recovery* and *The Cambridge History of African American Literature*. His works in progress include *Reading Race Reading America*, *Jazz South*, and *Richard Wright: One Reader's Responses*.

I am an outsider/insider Mississippian, the subject of other people's observations and the object of my reflections. Born in Washington, D.C., in 1943, I was repatriated in the late fall of 1949 to Moss Point, my father's hometown. My six-year-old self changed rapidly from being happy, carefree, and urban to being town-trapped, sullen, and confused. I could not understand why having an ice cream cone in the local drugstore was forbidden. So, this was Mississippi. A land of do-not-say-that and do-not- do-this. I was too young to sense the invisible segregation of the nation's capital and unprepared for the racism of the South and the permanent scar it would leave in my sensibility.

Even a six-year-old can have agency, however, even in 1950s Mississippi. I chose to keep, as much as I could, the speech patterns of my brief years in the North. You do not have to talk like a Mississippian to be one. I did not want to sound like my slow-talking cousins and older relatives, to sound like molasses creeping uphill on a cold day. The enervating drawl of the South did not appeal to me. I kept my vowels and my consonants and my distinct word-endings. I was teased for sounding "white." And by the measures used by my peers, I was odd for indulging my passion for reading, for wishing to be smart, as smart as my innately brilliant father and as well-mannered as my Louisiana-born mother, who insisted that *she* was not Negro but Creole and that *I* would not become food for the tragic appetites of Mississippi's white folks. The nightmares I had in 1955 about the lynching of Emmett Till assured me that she did not insist too much.

Unlike a few of our relatives, we did not have money. We were working-class, poor in pocket but rich in aspiration, sense of self-worth, dignity. I did not know we were poor. Poor people begged for things. We did not beg. If we asked for favors, we had to repay them. When my father's early retirement pension was not enough, my mother did domestic work. In my childhood imagination, I was an aristocrat exiled in a place called Mississippi. I was accustomed to the civilization of a bathroom. I resented having to learn the ritual of the outhouse and the art of bathing in a tin tub. I silently hated and resisted the low expectations most nonblack Mississippians had for black Mississippians and used my intellectual gifts to become who I am, a person for whom liking or disdaining Mississippi as home is a remarkably free choice.

The story of choice begs for a plot, a charting of a life history in which Mississippi is the home space for departures and returns. Perhaps plot can be an idiosyncratic almanac, an emotional structuring of time and place:

1943–1949—Washington, D.C.—Moss Point, Mississippi: The bliss of childhood was destroyed when my father took an early retirement for health reasons from his civil service job, and we moved from the city to the country in November 1949. My first Christmas in Mississippi was strange but not unpleasant. Eating oranges and apples in front of a fireplace and the pungent smell of a cedar Christmas tree is a decisive moment in becoming a Mississippian.

1949–1964—Moss Point—Tougaloo, Mississippi: These fifteen years are the longest continuous period of my claiming Mississippi as home, years that resonate the sorrow song of Richard Wright's *Black Boy* far more than the fantasia of Clifton Taulbert's *Once Upon a Time When We Were Colored*. Planting a pine tree when I was eight years old in our two-acre yard was a symbolic act of attaching myself to the soil, and it was and remains the symbiotic sign of self. That tree and I have survived dramatic changes of weather and social climate in Mississippi; it is the fixed point of the compass, the point to which I return in my mind no matter where my body might be. Whatever is Choctaw in my bloodline allows me to believe in the spirit of the tree and our primal entitlement to the land that time will restore to us.

The disadvantages of second-class citizenship in Mississippi killed any genuine feelings of patriotism I might have had for the United States and made me a loyal cynic in the Magnolia State. The false promises of American democracy as orchestrated in a sovereign closed society did, however, inspire me to be very serious about my education in public and parochial schools, and to be very receptive to a liberating education in mathematics, social responsibility, and life at Tougaloo College. There I embraced the ideals of Alpha Phi Alpha fraternity and transformed my private anger into the public assertions of the civil rights movement. Graduation from college was the beginning of six years of absence from home.

1964–1966—Chicago: Two years of working for a master's degree at Illinois Institute of Technology opened windows for seeing the joys and the horrors of urban experiences and for understanding that only New Orleans could meet my expectations of what urban life should be.

1966–1968—Albany, NY: Two years of work on English Renaissance literature at SUNY at Albany, of learning about diversity in the mindsets of New Yorkers.

1968–1970—United States Army, Fort Knox, KY, and Vietnam: Although I opposed the war, I was loyal to my country; on the other hand, my Asian exposure hardened my heart against the hypocrisy of America, against its casual, Aztec-like sacrificing of young men on the altars of the war gods.

1970–1974—Mississippi: I returned to teach at Tougaloo College.

1974–1977—Charlottesville, VA: I would serve my alma mater better if I had a terminal degree, so I went to the University of Virginia, wrote my dissertation, "Richard Wright and His American Critics, 1938–1960," and received the Ph.D. in 1978.

1977–1984—Mississippi: I returned to teaching at Tougaloo College, served for four years on the Mississippi Humanities Council, and chaired the Department of English, 1979-1986.

1985—Washington, D.C. The opportunity to return to the city of my birth and to work at the National Endowment for the Humanities as a program officer was a godsend.

1986–88—Mississippi: Teaching at Tougaloo College

1987–88—Alabama: UNCF Scholar-in-Residence at Talladega College

1988–1989—Mississippi: Teaching at Tougaloo College

1990–1991—Charlottesville, VA: Commonwealth Center for Literary and Cultural Change, UVA

1990—Publication of *Redefining American Literary History*

1992—Publication of *Black Southern Voices*

1991–2002—Mississippi: Teaching at Tougaloo College; Germany and France, 1993; United Kingdom and the British Museum, 1995

1996—Tennessee: Moss Chair of Excellence in English, University of Memphis

1997—Publication of *Trouble the Water: 250 Years of African American Poetry*

1999–2000—Chapel Hill, North Carolina: Fellow, National Humanities Center

2002–present—Louisiana: Distinguished Scholar and professor of English, Dillard University; epiphany in Senegal, 2004, and induction into the Tougaloo College Alumni Hall of Fame, 2009

2005–2006—Vicksburg, Mississippi: Exile after Hurricane Katrina and the breaking of the levees floods New Orleans

2008—Publication of *The Richard Wright Encyclopedia* and *THE KATRINA PAPERS: A Journal of Trauma and Recovery*

2009, 2010, 2011—Visits to China

2011—Richard Wright Literary Excellence Award and publication of *The Cambridge History of African American Literature*; designated a Famous Overseas Professor at Central China Normal University–Wuhan (2011–2014)

The vertical quality of the almanac represents ascent. Something, rather like the bark of the pine tree, conceals the horizontal, the growth rings, the outward movements that have an inner core. Like the tree, my life has been a process. The tree does not control changes in climate; it endures them even as it is changed by them, and so too have I been changed by the historical events that have reshaped Mississippi from 1949 to 2012. The concentric circles of my life are forever attached to Moss Point and Tougaloo College and the profound affinity I feel with the life and works of Richard Wright, *il miglior fabbro*. And there is also the rootedness in the soil of Mississippi. In my life, long teaching career, and writings, I have sought and still seek to fulfill a moral obligation: facing naked truths squarely and articulating them for a future.

Mary Ann Mobley

Mary Ann Mobley, Miss America 1959 from Brandon, Mississippi, has won many awards for work in the entertainment industry and for her work on behalf of war and famine victims. Her numerous honors include a Golden Globe Award from the Hollywood Foreign Press Association as "International Female Star of Tomorrow" (1965), Mississippi Woman of the Year (1979), the first woman voted into the University of Mississippi Alumni Hall of Fame (1981), and Mississippi Musicians Hall of Fame (2002). Mobley and her husband, Emmy award–winning talk show host Gary Collins, have one daughter, Mary Clancy.

I just can't do it—Lord knows I've tried! I've tried so many times and it just never seems to come out right no matter how hard I try or how long I anguish over it! I simply can't seem to put my feelings of home and Mississippi to paper. When you feel something so intensely, you *want* to write it down—if anguish to stanch the bleeding, if love or happiness to prolong the moment and share it. You want to let the ones who made it all possible, the ones who literally shaped your life know that you haven't forgotten them or their amazing gift of unconditional love. What is owed simply cannot be repaid. I am overwhelmed! Maybe if I pretend that we are all sitting here talking then I can just *tell* you.

I would tell you how the big cane rocking chair came to sit on the front porch of the house in Beverly Hills. It came from the porch at Stockett Stables. I used to sit and rock on that porch with "Mr. Robert." It was a wonderful gathering place where great stories as well as a few lies were freely swapped. Many people boarded their horses there, and it seemed that almost everybody stopped by at some time or another. The stories and the coffee never ran out, and magically there were always enough rocking chairs. I loved that man and will always miss him.

I can tell you about the love that surrounded me as I grew up in Brandon. At that time the population was around twenty-five hundred good people and a few old soreheads. It was not the kind of love that's talked about or analyzed, but the kind of love that's just there. It's like a physical condition that has no cure. It's a love that sits so comfortably and naturally deep inside you, never questioned, as I said, it's just there—like when my little dog, Prissy, was attacked by this big dog up the street. She was bleeding so badly and I wrapped her in one of mother's best towels and ran all the way up to our town square with her in my arms. I ran straight to Dr. Watson's office, past the receptionist and right into the examining room where he was seeing a patient. I stood there crying hysterically with Prissy bleeding in my arms. He simply said "excuse me" to the patient and gently guided me into the next examining room, put Prissy on the table, and proceeded to carefully stitch her up. When she was all bandaged, he wiped my face, gave me a hug (I think there's a huge shortage of hugs in our lives today), and then he called my mother to come get us. Did I mention that Dr. Watson wasn't a vet, but the doctor for most of the town of Brandon? This is a true story, as all my stories about home are true. You can't lie about things like that!

This was my growing-up place, where most everything revolved around the church and the school. I joined the church there, I was married there, and our daughter was baptized there.

If the church fed my soul, the school and my teachers fed my mind. From them you didn't just learn a subject, but you learned about life as well. To this day, I can remember most all of their names. I remember Miss Jessie Wilshire, who decided she couldn't teach us history until she taught us to write. She said she couldn't read our writing. So she taught us the old Palmer Penmanship Method where you go up to the top line, come down to the middle line. It's too complicated to explain, but years later, I almost fell out of bed one night when I heard

Johnny Carson on the old *Tonight Show* talking about having to learn the Palmer Penmanship Method of writing growing up in Nebraska. To this day, when people are nice enough to ask for my autograph, they often compliment my handwriting and I swear I think I see "Miss Jessie" smiling over their shoulder!

The next step in my life was truly monumental—how can I begin to tell you about my years at Ole Miss? If I'd had my way, I would have been a professional student there. I still think of going back. I would put my two rescue dogs, Brewster and Bailey, in the car and off we would go! I quite simply loved everything about my days there and I shudder to think that had it not been for one man, I would have missed one of the most extraordinary experiences of my life. My father had gone to Ole Miss and he must have had a great time because he insisted that my first two years at college be at a girl's school. However, George Street, who was director of Student Placement and Financial Aid, submitted my name for a new scholarship program donated by the Robert Carrier Foundation. I was so fortunate to be its first recipient and that's how I got to go to Ole Miss. It's inconceivable for me to think of my life without that experience. Sadly, most of the great men and women who touched my life there are no longer with us. They are gone but not forgotten: Chancellor Williams, Dean Hefley, Dean Malcolm Guess, and Dr. Noyes (we exchanged letters right up until his death a couple of years ago). Thankfully, I still have Dr. Pilkington and his lovely Lolly. He never gave me a perfect A. It was always an A- or a B+. Never a simple A. But I keep reminding him that he owes me one each time I see him.

I would probably still be in Oxford had it not been for the Miss America Pageant. Now, if you ever doubted that miracles can happen, look no further! This was a true Cinderella story about a short girl with a face as round as a MoonPie, but with the help of so many friends she ended up Miss America!

The Miss Mississippi Pageant was a blur. We had only two weeks to get me ready for Atlantic City. My gown came off the rack from either the Emporium or Kennington's and somehow I managed to come up with a talent act that still defies explanation to this day. I was so naïve.

Mary Taylor Sigman, the organist at Galloway Methodist Church, was incredibly kind; she wrote out the music for my talent on one piece of music manuscript paper—I didn't know I was supposed to have an orchestration! My Sunday school teacher, Miss Lona Aldridge, had made my talent costume and gave me a mustard seed bracelet, along with a card that quoted from the book of Matthew: "If ye have faith as a grain of mustard seed, . . . nothing shall be impossible unto you."

After that amazing year I used my Miss America scholarship to study in New York. I had always dreamed of one day being on Broadway. I was then twenty-two years old and my father thought I was too young to live on my own in the big city, so through the board of the Miss America Pageant, I found Norwood Baker, who became my roommate. Now I bet you are thinking this was a man—shame on you!

Nornie, as I called her, was from Spartanburg, South Carolina, and had been treasurer of Converse College before coming to New York to be the director of arts for the Association of American Colleges and Universities. She was one of those amazing southern women you were blessed to know. I learned so much from her. I even forgave her for dragging me to see so many James Joyce plays. Someone once said, and I believe it to be true, that "only God and James Joyce knew what James Joyce meant and sometimes even God wondered!"

However, one day she gave me one of the most enlightening gifts of my life. She introduced me to the writings of William Alexander Percy from the Mississippi Delta. His writing became incredibly special to me. Now this in no way negates my great love and admiration of Eudora Welty or our other great Mississippi writers of that time. Miss Eudora was a family friend and thrilled all of Southern California by graciously agreeing to be the commencement speaker at our daughter's graduation from Westlake School for Girls. She signed a copy of *One Writer's Beginnings* for each graduating senior. It was wonderful to visit with her. She loved honey baked ham and the occasional bottle of Maker's Mark.

Nor does this feeling diminish in any way the awe that swept over me when Mr. Blaylock introduced me that first time to William

Faulkner. It was in front of Blaylock Drug Store on the square in Oxford. From then on every time I saw Mr. Faulkner, he would raise his
hat to me and give me a very courteous "good afternoon, young lady," or
words to that effect.

I had not met wickedly wonderful Willie Morris yet, though what
great memories I have of him in later years. Some I can share and some
are best just enjoyed as I think back and laugh. I thank Willie for his
extraordinary talent and for introducing my mother to Dr. Verner
Smith Holmes! Dr. Holmes became "Poppa" and he was a saint, as he
had to be to marry into this family.

I am amazed when I think of all the brilliant and gifted writers that
my home state has produced. What an honor to have met so many of
them. I humbly salute them all. It's just that, at that time in my life,
William Alexander Percy was the one who opened a great door for
me. Through his writings he helped me understand all the new emotions I was experiencing. For the first time in my life I was a stranger
in a strange land called New York City, so very far from Brandon in so
many ways.

His book *Lanterns on the Levee* and his collection of poems seemed
to help me understand all the new emotions and contradictions I was
experiencing. He put everything that had eluded me into words.

He had been there before me. It was a different period in time, and
we had different dreams and different ambitions, but we both shared
that same pull back to the land that produced us and molded us.

I was excited by the city and all the famous people I was meeting. I
even got to live my dream of opening on Broadway. But it was Percy's
poem "Home" that kept it all in perspective. It played a tune on my
heart, and I can still recite it to this day. That's amazing because some
days I can't remember my own name.

New York was the beginning—my profession and good fortune
have given me the opportunity to travel to so many places in the world
and to meet people that I never thought I would meet. It allowed me
to see great sadness and cruelty in places like Cambodia during the fall
of Pol Pot. It made me see firsthand how unfair life can be when you
look in the faces of children dying of hunger, malnutrition, and disease.

I saw it not only in Cambodia, but in the Sudan, Somalia, Ethiopia, Zimbabwe and Mozambique, so many places. When it exists, I feel we need to see it and not look away. Then we must try to do something about it because we have a responsibility to try to make a difference. I was taught that in Brandon.

Now, not all has been sad; some has been beautiful and exciting. For a time we lived in Kenya where our daughter, Clancy, became fluent in Swahili. And for forty-three years, I have divided my time between a Cape Cod house with the proverbial white picket fence in California and our home in Jackson. I was lucky because I could always go home.

I know when I am home I can walk in my bare feet on the ground of my native land, in a place where I was born and where my bones will sleep, surrounded by my loved ones. For me, that place is Mississippi. When I bought the family burial plots, I bought an extra one under a struggling elm tree where I intend to put a bench. They have promised me that they will feed the tree, water it, give it vitamins, do whatever it takes to make it grow and become a real, regal southern shade tree. We may, however, have to work on our schedules; they have to have my tree ready when I move in.

Some have asked why I wanted all this—silly billies—I bet most of you know. It's so my friends can come and sit with me and visit for a while. We can have long talks, and they can tell me everything that's going on. Someone said it will be the first time that I won't be able to get the last word in.

I don't know if all this is unique to people who were born in Mississippi. Do people from other states feel the same way? Do they experience the same magnetic pull of home? I don't know, but I hope they do.

I think for most Mississippians, this is the question: do we ever really leave home, or is home simply inside of us wherever we go? I wonder . . .

I only know that like Will Percy . . .

> I have a need of silence and of stars;
> Too much is said too loudly; I am dazed.
> The silken sound of whirled infinity

Is lost in voices shouting to be heard.
I once knew men as earnest and less shrill.
An undermeaning that I caught I miss
Among these ears that hear all sounds save silence,
These eyes that see so much but not the sky,
These minds that gain all knowledge but no calm.
If suddenly the desperate music ceased,
Could they return to life? Or would they stand
In dancers' attitudes, puzzled, polite,
And striking vaguely hand on tired hand
For an encore, to fill the ghastly pause?
I do not know. Some rhythm there may be
I cannot hear. But I—oh, I must go
Back where the breakers of deep sunlight roll
Across flat fields that love and touch the sky;
Back to the more of earth, the less of man,
Where there is still a plain simplicity,
And friendship, poor in everything but love,
And faith, unwise, unquestioned, but a star.
Soon now the peace of summer will be there
With cloudy fire of myrtles in full bloom;
And, when the marvelous wide evenings come,
Across the molten river one can see
The misty willow-green of Arcady.
And then—the summer stars . . . I will go home.

For me, that says it all.

Acknowledgments

The editors are deeply indebted to each of the writers represented in this collection who responded promptly to our various requests for memories, bios, and photographs. We understand all too well that they had to make time in their packed schedules to pause and reflect, pull and reassemble the past, shape into words and share on paper their very personal stories about the circumstances that led them to leave Mississippi and the series of events that led them to "come on back," as Willie Morris says. In addition, we thank Craig Gill, Lelia Salisbury, and the outstanding staff at University Press of Mississippi for their excellent counsel, guidance, support, and skilled involvement with this project. We also wish to thank James Patterson for his willingness to share his talent and expert help in all things related to photography. Special thanks are due to Gloria Vanderbilt and Anderson Cooper for their permission to reprint from Wyatt Cooper's classic work, to JoAnne Prichard Morris and David Rae Morris for allowing us to use Willie Morris's fine essay, to William O. Luckett, Jr., for obtaining Morgan Freeman's permission to reprint his work, and to Jeffrey A. Varas for allowing us to reprint Barry Hannah's work.

Copyright Acknowledgments

COPYRIGHT ACKNOWLEDGMENTS

Photography Credits

Wyatt Cooper – Jack Robinson/Cooper-Vanderbilts Archive
 Photos/Getty Images
Bob Allan Dunaway – by Mary Lynn Dunaway
William Dunlap – by Carol Harrison
Morgan Freeman – by James Patterson
Carolyn Haines – by John Adams, Adams Imaging
Barry Hannah – by Charline McCord
Mary Donnelly Haskell – by Mary Ann Halpin
Sam Haskell – by Mary Ann Halpin
William Jeanes – by Kinkajou Studios
Russell Knight – by Julie Arthur
Johnnie Mae Maberry – by DJ Green
Charline R. McCord – by James Patterson
Jo McDivitt – by Brent Wallace
Willie Morris – by Kay Holloway
Ronnie Riggs – by Charline McCord
Maureen Ryan – by Tracy Liles
David Sheffield – by Cynthia Walker
Scott Stricklin – by Russ Houston
Keith Thibodeaux – by ImageWise Photography
J. Dale Thorn – by Jean Lively
Judy H. Tucker – by James Patterson
Cynthia Walker – by David Sheffield
Tricia Walker – by Tony Phipps Photography
Jerry W. Ward, Jr. – by McNeal Cayette

Jesmyn Ward – by John Adams, Adams Imaging
Sela Ward – Courtesy CBS
Norma Watkins – by Les Cizek
Dolphus Weary – Courtesy of InterVarsity Christian Fellowship
(IVCF) Board of Trustees, 2011